KU-760-244

CONTENTS

[3]

FOREWORD

Transport in Britain, as in many other countries, is a politicised market. The railways are state-owned and in the rest of the market state intervention is rife. Inevitably, pressure groups flourish, seeking government support which benefits their members whilst imposing the costs on others. It is hardly surprising that there are always 'transport problems' and that they are perceived to require even more government action.

Yet government action seems to have been ineffective: there is no sign that Britain's transport problems have lessened over the years. The country is bedevilled by a long-standing problem of road congestion in urban areas (especially London) and on certain motorways, which is a consequence of the absence of any pricing system (varied by area and by time of day) which faces road users with the costs of their consumption of road space. For years governments have attempted to solve this problem only from the supply side, assuming that if some roads are congested the answer is to build more roads. The only significant demand-side measure to reinforce this self-defeating policy has arisen from the (incidental) effects of increases in taxes on fuel.

Competition with the state-owned railways, which have to pay their track costs, has been distorted. The railways are run-down, heavily subsidised, apparently facing further decline and, according to many claims, starved of investment. But in the absence of a market in transport, there is no way of judging what that investment 'should' be.

Nevertheless, as Professor John Hibbs points out in Hobart Paper No.121, hopeful signs are appearing. Privatisation and deregulation of buses have gone a long way, rail privatisation is now firmly on the agenda, and Ministers have begun openly to discuss road pricing.

Professor Hibbs will have none of the calls for a 'long-term co-ordinated transport policy' which, in practice, means a yet more politicised transport sector. Instead, he favours market solutions to Britain's transport problems. He wants consumers' decisions to be made '...within a market which extends to all forms of physical mobility' (VI, p.89). He begins with an overview of transport modes; in Sections III and IV he examines in detail two areas in which he is one of Britain's leading experts - the consequences of bus deregulation and road-use pricing ('an idea whose time has come'); and in Sections V and VI he sets out his policy conclusions.

Many people will be particularly interested in Professor Hibbs's discussion of bus deregulation and privatisation. This form of transport, for years regarded as lowly and plagued by 'public' owners with no incentive to cater for consumers' demands, has experienced a burst of innovation since deregulation. As the dead hand of 'public' ownership has been removed, a process of discovery has begun, leading to innovation in technology and management. There is a long way to go, and inevitably some of the new owners will fail, but at least change is occurring.

Professor Hibbs observes that some local authorities still try to indulge their passion for expensive solutions to transport problems, favouring systems such as LRT (Light Rapid Transit, translated by Hibbs as 'Love Running Trams'). He envisages consumer requirements being met more flexibly and cheaply by innovative bus systems such as KGB (Kerb Guided Buses). Hibbs also argues persuasively that it is particularly important, to avoid distortion of investment decisions across the whole transport industry, that road pricing should be introduced as soon as possible. As he says, 'Since roads do not really belong to anyone, it is not surprising that they are used wastefully' (IV, p.70). He believes the regulation of taxis (including hire cars) is also out of date so that radical reform is required.

The Institute of Economic Affairs has no corporate view. Statements made in its publications are those of the author, not of the Institute's Trustees, Advisers or Directors. It offers Professor Hibbs's stimulating views on road transport policy as essential reading for transport policy-makers, all those concerned about government failure in transport, and everyone who wishes to see the system improved.

April 1993   COLIN ROBINSON
Editorial Director, Institute of Economic Affairs;
Professor of Economics, University of Surrey

THE AUTHOR

JOHN HIBBS is Emeritus Professor of Transport Management at the University of Central England in Birmingham. After some years in road and rail transport, he began his academic career at the then City of London College, and he has sought in all his writing and teaching to keep in touch with the people who run the business of moving people and goods. Apart from two previous *Hobart Papers* (referred to in the text), his publications include *The History of British Bus Services* (1968, 2nd edn., 1989), *The Country Bus* (1986), as well as several textbooks on transport management and marketing. He is currently Editor of the *Proceedings* of the Chartered Institute of Transport, and Chairman of the Roads and Road Transport History Conference.

ACKNOWLEDGEMENTS

The encouragement of Professors Geoffrey Wood and Colin Robinson made me feel that the subject was worth exploring, and developing from my previous Hobarts. In discussing an earlier draft with Professor Michael Beesley I reached certain further conclusions which have I hope strengthened the argument. My colleagues Ian Dickins and Mike Waterhouse have made valuable contributions, without necessarily agreeing with my arguments. I am also indebted to innumerable friends, including many of my own students, who have argued with me and challenged my position as often as they have agreed with it. Particular thanks in this context must go to my fellow-members of the Organisation of Teachers of Transport Studies. And, as with all my work in this field, I gratefully acknowledge the initial impetus to study transport regulation, which came from the late Gilbert Ponsonby.

I need hardly add that responsibility for any errors of fact or interpretation and for the paper's conclusions, remains solely my own.

March 1993   J.H.

I. INTRODUCTION

Mobility and Modernisation

Kipling remarked 'transport is civilisation', meaning that trade and transport are essential to economic growth and a flourishing economy. Yet, in the empires of antiquity and in more recent examples, fear that the free movement of people might undermine the established social order led to the regulation and control of the means whereby such movement might expand. Thus this great engine of modernisation became feared and distrusted by those who see change and growth and the challenge of liberty as threats. It is not surprising that Max Weber regarded the provision of transport as a function of the bureaucratic state.[1]

In Britain, the Tudor Settlement (widely taken to be the start of 'modern history') enabled a travel industry to emerge. But the hackney carriage, which appeared about 1625, was regarded as effete—'real men ride horseback'—and the stage coaches which began to cover the kingdom a generation later were similarly suspect. The volume of movement was then small in comparison with that made possible by railways 200 years later which incurred the strong disapproval of the Duke of Wellington who feared riots and civil disorder.

The 19th century saw a rapid growth of traffic which, continuing through the 20th century, has given us a mobile society unparalleled in history. But those who distrust modernisation have always feared that greater mobility threatened all they had come to accept as desirable in the world about them. So the railway became a symbol of past security, endangered by attempts by Dr Beeching and others to bring it up to date, and the motor car (and, still worse, the motorway) brought out atavistic fears of where it might lead. Perhaps such fears are the underlying cause of the emotionalism that characterises the debate about the private car, and not least the vociferous contributions of the 'anti-car' lobby.

---

[1] M. Weber, *Wirtschaft und Gesellschaft*, quoted in H.H. Gerth and C. Wright Mills, *From Max Weber: Essays in Sociology*, London: Kegan Paul, Trench, Trubner & Co., 1947.

Personal Mobility Highly Valued in the Modern World

But personal mobility is much valued in the late 20th century. Ownership of personal transport is desired from an early age, for it ensures the achievement of sought-after ends. Thus the car becomes a symbol of personal maturity for the young, and of independence for the more mature adults and even the elderly. In contrast, public transport (the aeroplane apart) is seen as an inferior good. Perhaps as a consequence there is a political polarisation which results in support for the car being seen as 'right-wing' while public transport is the intellectual property of socialists. Consequently, discussion of a very serious issue is inhibited.

Ironically, the growth of personal mobility through car ownership seems to be reaching its limits, since it causes wasteful and frustrating congestion. Car ownership is now a central political issue. However, many of the controversies about transport policy are primarily the result of decades of intervention and regulation which have fragmented the market for mobility, in which the satisfaction of demand is set about with distortions of every kind.

Mobility in the Market

Some regard mobility as a right, and seek to measure it in order to 'top up' its availability to certain people. Attempts at measurement are merely scientistic,[2] producing no useful data because the degree of mobility which maximises the marginal utility of one person can only be judged subjectively by that person, in the context of alternative satisfactions, prices in the market and available spending power. This *Hobart Paper* seeks to define conditions in which the market process, involving the various modes of transport, can bring supply and demand into better balance. But we must acknowledge the powerful emotions that the subject can evoke, particularly among those who distrust the market process as an agent of change. Such reactions are understandable. T.S. Eliot expressed them in the 1930s in words as apt today as they were then:

---

[2] 'Scientism', which Hayek prefers to call 'constructivist rationalism', falsely concludes that Cartesian rules of scientific method can provide the necessary information for decisions about the allocation of scarce resources. In this he follows Popper (K.R. Popper, *The Logic of Scientific Discovery*, London: Hutchinson, 1959).

'And no man knows or cares who is his neighbour
Unless his neighbour makes too much disturbance,
But all dash to and fro in motor cars,
Familiar with the roads and settled nowhere.'
(*Choruses from 'The Rock'*, 1934)

II. THE MEANS TO MOBILITY: AN OVERVIEW OF METHODS OF TRANSPORT

Public Transport and the Private Car

When transport policy is debated, 'public transport' is distinguished from 'the private car'. The same distinction exists in Transport Studies in the universities, so that sometimes the car appears not to be part of the transport industry at all. Yet in Britain in 1991, 86 per cent of passenger-miles involved travel by car or taxi, against 7 per cent by bus or coach, 6 per cent by train, and 1 per cent by motor cycle, pedal cycle and aircraft.[1] Table 1 shows the same preference for car travel in terms of individual journeys. To the dispassionate observer it must seem strange that textbooks use so much space in discussion of the economics and management of trains and buses, and so little on the dominant form of transport.

Relative Costs

There are, of course, basic differences between the economics of public transport and the economics of running a car, the most obvious being the relatively small labour costs of the latter. The labour element in public road passenger transport accounts for some 60 per cent of costs.[2] But for a capable do-it-yourself mechanic, the apparent labour element (excluding the value of his own time) in running his car is limited to the labour input into the manufacture of necessary spare parts and into the production and distribution of fuel, lubricants and tyres. The middle-class driver who depends upon a motor agency to service his car will have much higher out-of-pocket costs since he is paying for the time of others. At one time, the use of chauffeurs represented another significant labour input into car use but, company cars apart, few chauffeurs are now employed.

---

[1] *Transport Statistics Great Britain 1992*, London: HMSO, 1992, Table 1.1.

[2] *Bus Industry Monitor 1992*, Preston: Transport Advisory Service, 1992, p.38. Wage costs, per employee and as a proportion of total costs, were lower than average in the former state-owned companies.

The full costs of running a car are probably such that bus or train travel is cheaper, per passenger-mile, if the driver is the sole passenger.[3] British Rail offers market-based fares over some routes that compare very favourably with the out-of-pocket costs of car travel, particularly when city-centre parking places/prices have to be found. Public transport is poor in rural areas but there are few journeys in towns (except on Sundays) that cannot

TABLE 1

JOURNEYS PER PERSON PER WEEK IN GREAT BRITAIN:
BY MODE OF TRANSPORT, 1985-86

Main mode of transport		No. of Journeys per week
CAR:	Driver	5·60
	Passenger	3·50
	Total car	9·11
TRAIN:	British Rail	0·22
	London Underground	0·11
	Total train	0·33
BUS:	London Buses	0·22
	Other local (stage) bus	1·34
	Total bus	1·56
OTHER:	Other public transport[1]	0·17
	Cycle	0·31
	Motorcycle	0·15
	Private hire bus or coach	0·17
	Other private transport[2]	0·06
	Total 'Other'	0·86
WALK (over 1 mile)		1·37
TOTAL ALL MODES		13·22

Notes: [1] Probably express coach services.
[2] Probably vans, personnel carriers, etc.
Source: Transport Statistics Great Britain 1991,
London: HMSO, 1991, Table 1.3(a).

[3] See J. Hibbs, *The Bus and Coach Industry, its Economics and Organisation,* London: J.M. Dent, 1975, pp.99-102.

be made by bus. For inter-urban travel, express coach services offer prices well below the cost of similar journeys by car, even where a passenger is being carried.

But while public transport firms must cover all their costs, private motorists tend to follow different accounting procedures. Motorists tend to treat virtually all costs other than fuel as fixed in the short term. Few take account of the opportunity cost of the capital tied up in the car (let alone that of the garage in which it is kept—if such there be). Insurance can be paid by monthly direct debit, and when it comes to tax, and even replacement, many people probably 'live in hope'. Even fuel may be regarded as a fixed cost when deciding whether or not to use the car, so long as there is sufficient petrol in the tank.

Thus the *perceived* cost of car use is a small part of the actual private costs involved, and contains no element of externalities. At the same time, the cost of public transport is perceived to be higher than its money price (because of its relative inconvenience). Moreover, the public transport fare may not be known: although coaches and trains compete to some extent on price, bus companies are for some reason loth to publicise their fares. The motorist is, of course, not behaving irrationally, for once a car has been acquired and a large part of its cost is sunk, it is reasonable to compare it with public transport on the basis of what may be called *generalised cost*.

To take a familiar example, when contemplating a journey from home to the office or the shopping centre there are obvious disutilities in using public transport. To go by public transport will involve *walking* to the station or the bus stop; *waiting* for the train or bus to arrive; quite possibly *changing*, with further walking and waiting; and finally *walking* to the destination. While the scale of these disutilities will vary from person to person, along with the distances and the state of the weather, there is a real cost in waiting, with its uncertainty,[4] and even a sense of inferiority as cars pass the bus stop. It is hardly surprising that most of those who can afford it use the car, even at the cost of forgoing other satisfactions. The remarkable thing is the failure of public transport, and bus companies in particular, to develop an effective marketing reaction.

---

[4] The train may offer greater security in this sense than the bus, and even the presence of tramlines in the road is visual proof that a vehicle is likely to come along.

Although some slogans, like 'Travel by bus—less parking fuss', date from the 1960s, when car ownership was starting to expand, little attention was paid to the quality of the product, and no attempt was made to use price as a marketing weapon since the licensing system forbade it. Yet the first fruits of regulatory reform, the development of the urban minibus, showed that people could be persuaded to shift from the car to the bus. Where local authorities have given buses some degree of priority, this too has proved attractive to passengers. The problem is that the bus industry, cocooned in a licensing system which (it was supposed) had put an end to competition, realised almost too late that its true competitor was the private car.

Non-Monetary Satisfactions

Car ownership, on the other hand, offers various non-monetary satisfactions. For example, there is a general increase in liberty. Not for nothing was possession of a 'Trabant' car symbolic of freedom for many who lived under the former East German tyranny. For those who would otherwise face a shopping trip by bus, with small children to look after, a car is clearly preferable. The ability to respond to family emergencies both quickly and effectively is another advantage of having a car in front of the house.

There are other such benefits, too, in terms of convenience and security. For anyone working late on a winter evening, the prospect of waiting in the snow for public transport has to be set against the alternative of a car waiting in the car park: the price differential would need to be substantial to make public transport attractive in such circumstances. The journey, too, is perceived to be safer, driving through the streets with doors locked against hostile strangers. Even in the face of severe congestion, it is understandable that many people will prefer the ambience of the car, with a choice of music to pass the time, to the relative austerity of bus, tube, train or tram.

Valuation of time saved is difficult,[5] but there is no doubt that access to a car offers the possibility of greater satisfaction in the course of a day than could be obtained by the use of public transport. So it may be entirely rational for individuals and firms to decide that such non-monetary benefits outweigh the money

---

[5] It can be argued that the aggregation of small quantities of time supposed to be saved, as used in cost/benefit calculations for road investment, is of very little real significance or value.

cost of keeping a car—as our forefathers doubtless decided when looking at the cost of maintaining a horse and carriage.

Unfortunately, some public transport managers seem to have accepted all too readily the image of the industry as a supplier of an inferior good, to be used by people who can afford nothing better, so that public transport inevitably declines as incomes increase. Far worse, many local authorities have concurred, choosing to subsidise public transport, failing to understand that producer-subsidy tends to inhibit innovation and development of a market response to the competition of the car. Moreover, the image of public transport itself reflects the poor quality of customer care that its providers have seen fit for so long to offer. Studies suggest[6] a general agreement among bus passengers that frequency and reliability rank highest in their assessment of quality. Yet the number of companies that have failed to use the urban minibus in order to maximise these qualities seems to suggest a blind 'machismo' that says 'real men drive double-deckers'. Too many of these macho bus drivers fail to give their passengers a chance to reach their seats before pulling away, let alone making them feel 'welcome aboard'. Power-assisted steering, which makes it easier to drive a bus, can make it less pleasant to ride in. Even the official recommendations for more user-friendly vehicles, from the Disabled Passengers Transport Advisory Committee (DiPTAC), do nothing to change the austere and uninviting interiors of most contemporary buses, which compare badly with the homelike comfort of the private car.

The Car and Transport Policy

Another non-monetary satisfaction deriving from car ownership is the value of the car as a status symbol. For example, the allocation to employees of fleet cars which increase in cost with increases in status, makes little sense in terms of providing a means of getting those employees from place to place at minimum expense but it provides them with visible symbols of status. The 'cascading'[7] of the bigger cars through the used car market brings powerful vehicles within the reach of many potential car-owners[8] in the lower income brackets.

[6] See L. Pickup *et al.*, *Bus Deregulation in the Metropolitan Areas*, Aldershot: Avebury, Oxford Studies in Transport, 1991, Ch.13.

[7] 'Cascading' is a term used in public transport to indicate the process of repositioning vehicles when new rolling stock is acquired for premium services.

[8] See Table 2, below, p.22.

The market will adjust to the presence of superior goods such as the car. But the motor car industry itself has an unusual status which public transport lacks. Consequently, politicians have placed the car in a different régime from other forms of transport. The car industry's contribution to the domestic product is matched by its importance for the export of goods and by the employment it provides. Market distortions include protection of the domestic industry by artificially inflated prices for imported cars and the treatment of company cars for tax purposes. However, it is the car as 'sacred cow' that inhibits all attempts to discuss it as a transport policy issue. The UK government has a Minister of State for Public Transport, but you will search *Whitaker* in vain for his opposite number for the private car. For a government to seek genuine competitive markets in the manufacture, import, taxation and distribution of motor cars—which is where the worst distortions in the market for mobility originate—would take prodigious political courage.

Regulatory Policy

Regulatory policy also treats different modes of transport unequally. The enforcement of higher safety standards for public transport is matched by significantly lower accident levels. In the decade 1980-1990, deaths per billion passenger kilometres were 4·9 for cars, 0·9 for trains, and 0·6 for buses and coaches. The figures are stark though they are generally ignored. The reason is plain: some 60 per cent of the population hold a full driving licence, rising to more than 90 per cent in the 'professional' class. Each of us tends to assume that she or he is a good driver—it is always 'the other chap' who is to blame. But the standards of competence required of car drivers are poor when compared with the standards set for drivers of trains or heavy commercial vehicles.

It is surely remarkable that any civilised society should tolerate injury and death on such a scale, but there is reason to expect that the necessary reforms would have a wider beneficial effect. Enforcing standards of competence, for example, would avoid the absurd situation in which someone can pass an inadequate test with minimum experience, limited to the use of a small car on urban streets, and then drive a powerful car, at night, on a busy road or motorway. From press and broadcasting we hear all too frequently of fatalities arising from 'loss of control of the car' by young and inexperienced drivers: this must suggest that current standards of competence required of drivers fail to ensure adequate road skills. Holding a driving licence for a heavy goods or passenger-carrying vehicle[9] confers status, and its loss places the driver's employment at risk. The driving licence for cars, on the other hand, is seen almost as a right, such is the pressure for individual mobility in our society.

Measures taken under the Road Traffic Act 1992 will go some way to deal with the after-effects of permitting incompetent or irresponsible drivers to take to the road. But even were access to car use made harder, underlying distortions would remain in the way such use is paid for: payments for road use and the case for electronic road pricing are addressed in Section IV.

Another issue arises from the sumptuary nature of much of the relevant taxation, and the distaste of the Treasury for any hypothecation of tax revenue.[10] The taxation of road users, like the taxation of alcohol and tobacco, is designed to take advantage of the inelasticity of demand with respect to price. In recent years it has taken on the further function, as have the tobacco and alcohol taxes, of seeking to regulate consumption in line with unquantifiable social or environmental objectives. It may be thought foolish for government to neglect such a reliable source of revenue, even if it seems improper for VAT to be levied on the even more inelastic demand for food.[11] But there are many inconsistencies and distortions in the transport tax régime, such as exemption of railways from tax (other than VAT) on their energy supplies, and rebate of fuel tax to operators of

[9] The former is familiar as the 'HGV', while the 'PCV' has replaced the previous, and better-known, 'PSV' licence.

[10] The compiler of *The Oxford Companion to Law* takes an agreeably critical attitude to taxation as a practice: 'Traditionally the principal way in which the ruling classes in organised communities have oppressed, fleeced and expropriated some of their subjects', he calls it, and goes on to say that 'Neither justice nor reason has any place in tax law, and many decisions of the superior courts are in plain conflict with all sense and reason'. With such an authority—that of the Regius Professor of Law in the University of Glasgow—we may dispose of any notion that what road users pay in taxation is related in a meaningful way to the benefits they obtain. (D.M. Walker, *The Oxford Companion to Law*, OUP, 1980.)

[11] VAT, as well as fuel tax, is of course levied on the *distribution* of foodstuffs at every stage from farm to supermarket.

local bus services, but not to those running express coaches in competition with British Rail.

Making Sense of the Car

Despite the moralising of the anti-car lobby (not to be confused with the public transport lobby), demand for personal mobility will undoubtedly remain high, and not just among the middle classes. As the Introduction explains, there is an unfortunate tendency for the car to be seen as the 'property' of the right wing in politics, and for public transport to belong to the left. A more balanced view is suggested by the statistics in Table 2 which show how far car ownership has penetrated every level of society increasingly over the past decade. In 1989/90, 43 per cent of 'unskilled manual' households had the regular use of a car, as did 84 per cent of 'skilled manual' households, the latter approaching the 95

TABLE 2

HOUSEHOLDS WITH REGULAR USE OF ONE
OR MORE CARS:
MANUAL SOCIO-ECONOMIC GROUPS, GREAT BRITAIN,
1982-1990
(Percentages)
(No. of households (millions) in brackets)

| Year | Socio-economic group | | |
	Skilled manual[1]	Semi-skilled manual[2]	Unskilled manual
1982/84	73 (5·0)	42 (2·8)	30 (0·8)
1984/86	77 (5·1)	50 (2·9)	35 (0·8)
1985/87	79 (5·2)	56 (2·9)	38 (0·8)
1988	82 (4·7)	60 (1·8)	47 (0·4)
1989/90	84 (4·6)	62 (1·8)	43 (0·4)

Notes: [1] Includes foremen, farm managers, and own account workers.
          [2] Includes personal service workers and farm workers.

Source: General Household Surveys, OPCS, Social Survey Division, London: HMSO, 1990.

[22]

per cent found among 'employers and managers' and 'professional' people.[12]

Clearly the car is no longer a middle-class luxury. In so far as it greatly widens the opportunity of finding employment, it is of considerable social and economic significance. Moreover, ownership is no longer limited to the young and middle-aged. A trend which is significant for public transport is that more people are continuing to drive later in life: between 1975 and 1990 the number of people aged 70 or over holding a full driving licence doubled, to 30 per cent of the age group.[13]

The extent of car ownership means no government is likely to take draconian measures against car use. One alternative is to harmonise the fiscal and regulatory régimes which apply to the car with those for other forms of passenger transport.

Development of the Taxi

As passenger transport has developed, it has become cheaper, leading to the increased availability of mobility for more and more people. Typically, as in the case of airlines, larger vehicles have enabled fixed costs to be spread over a growing payload, thereby reducing unit costs. In rail and air transport alike, this tendency has in the past been sufficient to offset increased investment and higher operating costs, and has therefore reduced fares, in real terms, so stimulating demand. The spread of car ownership is the most recent example; the cheapening that has followed from long production lines for a few standard models has made the private car a form of mass transport.

The first steps in this process were taken about 1625, when it was realised there was a market for coach travel among people who could not afford the substantial cost of 'keeping a carriage'. The secret was to carry more people, and the method came to be called *plying for hire*. We can only guess at the originator, but he seems to have been a Londoner, for the vehicles came to be called 'Hackney Carriages', the term which still applies to all vehicles that ply for hire on the streets.

The taxi is thus the earliest mode of public transport, which may account for the peculiarities of its regulatory régime.

---

[12] *Transport Statistics Great Britain 1991*, London: HMSO, 1991.

[13] *Transport Statistics Great Britain 1991, ibid.* The proportion for women was only 13 per cent. The compilers counsel the use of caution on account of a relatively small sample, but the figures illustrate the general trend.

It is a world-wide phenomenon, and in some countries the predominant mode. In the many varieties of 'jitney' to be found where state regulations permit, its function overlaps that of the bus, but it is not unusual for taxis (or hire cars) to be driven by their owners, and for people to drift into and out of the trade.

In Britain, outside London, the 'cruising' taxi is uncommon, most cabs being hired at a rank or pre-booked by telephone. The popular image of the taxi as an up-market form of transport is also inappropriate outside central London, for sharing the fare makes the cost to the individual similar to that for a comparable bus journey. Add to this the convenience of being able to pile the shopping and the kids into a cab on the High Street rank, and it is easy to see the comparative attraction of the taxi, which also saves the cost of parking the car. Hire cars and taxis are also used for holiday journeys, access to airports and for emergency trips, where they compete with the train and the express coach. The taxi has come to be the people's motor car.

Statistics about taxis and hire cars in Britain are limited, but the latest figures[14] record that taxis in London increased from 12,600 in 1981 to 16,500 10 years later, and licensed drivers from 17,800 to 20,600 over the same period. Outside London the number of taxis rose from 17,400 to 20,600 in the decade. There is no information about the number of hire cars, often still called minicabs.

The subject is delicate, since the right to ply for hire on the street (generally, in practice, on a rank) is a privilege jealously defended by the taxi trade, with occasions of violence when 'unlicensed' minicab drivers have attempted to overstep the law. Yet the distinction between the taxi and the hire car is legal rather than practical, and the case for a unified régime is strong.[15] Feelings run high, however, and the recommendations of this *Hobart Paper* (below, pp. 28-29) will no doubt be unwelcome to the taxi trade.

The regulatory régime for London taxis differs from that in force elsewhere.[16] In the London Taxi Area the Public

---

[14] *Transport Statistics Great Britain 1992, op. cit.*

[15] The so-called London taxi or 'black cab' is not a taxi within the meaning of the legislation, although in some cities such vehicles are the only ones acceptable to the local authority for the issue of a licence.

[16] On the economics of the London taxi trade, with its high level of contestability, see 'Competition and supply in London taxis', in M.E. Beesley, *Privatisation, Regulation and Deregulation*, London: IEA in association with Routledge, 1992.

Carriage Office (PCO), an agency of the Metropolitan Police, is the licensing authority for the black cabs, but has no jurisdiction over minicabs. The PCO's authority lies in the Metropolitan Public Carriage Act 1869: only cabs licensed under that Act may ply for hire on the streets and ranks of the Area. Elsewhere in England and Wales (and for hire cars in London) the licensing authority is the District Council, under the Town Police Clauses Act 1847; for Scotland the Civic Government (Scotland) Act applies. The Town Police Clauses powers were adoptive (that is, they had to be adopted by resolution of the council), but the Transport Act 1985 extended them to all areas of all District Councils.

Originally the 1847 Act applied to buses and coaches as well as cabs, but its powers were thought to be inappropriate in the 1920s, and it was superseded by the Road Traffic Act 1930. The 1985 Act did no more than to bring the regulation of cabs in the provinces to a position like that reached for public service vehicles 55 years earlier. An opportunity was lost there to give parity of treatment to every kind of hackney carriage.

Taxis and Hire Cars

The taxi enjoys a privileged position when compared to the hire car. It is also (especially in London) harder to enter the licensed taxi trade than it is to enter the hire car business. In London, as is well known, taxi drivers have to acquire 'the knowledge' which means passing a searching examination of the geography of the London Taxi Area before a licence is issued. Some provincial cities have recently introduced similar tests, but they are rare. To drive a hire car, it is only necessary to hold a clean driving licence. The result is a two-tier profession, with much animosity between cabbies and minicab drivers.

Yet the difference is increasingly artificial, for advances in information technology have made the significance of plying for hire obsolete, except for the use of limited space on ranks. Hire cars can and usually do carry radio-telephones, so that a prospective customer can call the office to book the car almost as readily as one can book a taxi by agreement with the driver, and taxi firms take telephone bookings just like their hire car competitors. The case for a unified régime seems clear.

There is, however, a safety issue. When hackneys first appeared it was possible for the hirer to form a reasonable assessment of the quality of the vehicle and the horse. Such an assessment is not possible with a motor vehicle, so some form of quality control is needed, applied to any type of vehicle submitted for approval by a licensing authority.

The more interesting question is how far quantity or price control may be required. Since both have been abandoned for buses and coaches it is hard to see why other hackney carriages should form a special case. Limiting the number of licensed cabs creates a monopoly for the fortunate few. Thus control of quantity may appear to justify control of price. In a reasonably contestable market it is competition that prevents extortionate pricing. But competition is not appealing to the fortunate few, or to those who aspire to that status.

Price control of licensed taxis is common; it is often defended on the grounds that people would be confused by different fares quoted by different drivers on the same rank. Authorised fares seem to vary from city to city,[17] though there is little evidence that they are correlated with the presence or absence of quantity control. Price control does not apply to hire cars, but in the absence of data it may be assumed that the market tends to equate their charges with those of the licensed trade.

Monopoly Value of Licensed Cabs

Prior to the partial reforms of 1985, evidence shows that the monopoly value of a licensed cab was substantial.[18] Nine pairs of cities and towns were examined, each pair being comparable in size and in social and demographic characteristics. In each case it was found, as one would expect, that the more limited was the number of licences available, the higher was the value of a cab. It follows that restrictions on the supply of taxis permitted to ply for hire prior to 1985 increased monopoly profits and stimulated competition in the form of the growth of the hire car trade. The latter had been subjected to quality control by the Local Government (Miscellaneous Provisions) Act 1976, which enabled councils

---

[17] See G.A. Coe & R.L. Jackson, *Some new evidence relating to quantity control in the taxi industry*, Crowthorne, Berks: Transport & Road Research Laboratory, 1983.

[18] *Ibid.*, pp. 17-20.

to adopt appropriate powers, but did not permit restrictions on the issue of licences. Nor did it permit price control, since prospective customers were expected to 'shop around' before booking a car.

The Transport Act 1985 attempted no radical reform of taxi and hire car legislation. Apart from extending existing taxi licensing to all areas, it permitted a taxi to be hired at separate fares, but only where a council made a 'scheme'.[19] It did attempt to encourage 'taxibus' services, which had been expected to develop after the reform of bus licensing, but hedged them around with new regulations which made their operation unnecessarily complicated. By the end of May 1987, 76 taxi operators had registered 99 local bus services.[20]

In the politically delicate area of quantity control of licensed taxis the 1985 Act contained provisions that suggest a compromise between the vested interests of the cab trade, the desire of councils to retain their powers, and the aims of the Department of Transport to achieve regulatory reform. The result, as encoded in Section 16 of the Act, reads as follows:

> '...the grant of a licence (for a taxi) may be refused, for the purposes of limiting the number of hackney carriages in respect of which licences are granted, if, but only if, the person authorised to grant licences is satisfied that there is no significant demand for the services of hackney carriages (within the area to which the licence would apply) which is unmet.'

Since, in a reasonably contestable market, it is to be assumed that supply will tend over time to equate with demand, the implication is that a council may only limit the number of licences it issues if there is no need to do so! But after the Act came into force 'a number of councils attempted to quantify (the unmet) demand',[21] which implies seeking to prove a negative. Unsurprisingly, the researcher concludes: 'Reports of several of the surveys have been studied—none have

---

[19] 'The circumstances known as splitting a taxi', as the Road Traffic Act 1937 put it, have troubled legislators since the introduction of quantity control, and the bus industry has never favoured the idea of taxi passengers paying separate fares. They will, of course, whether or not it be legal.

[20] D.J. Finch, *The impact of the 1985 Transport Act on the taxi industry*, Crowthorne, Berks: Transport & Road Research Laboratory, 1988.

[21] Finch, *op. cit.*, p.3.

provided a final measure of potential "unmet" demand'. For surely the absurdity of the situation lies in the likelihood that any 'unmet' demand will be catered for by the hire car firms, who are active in the same market.

So useful and widely used a contributor to personal mobility should surely be something more than the Cinderella of public transport. Nothing should be done to raise the investment threshold unduly, or to discourage the owner-driver (known in the London cab trade as a 'musher'). Price control, if it leads to increased fares, will be self-defeating.

A Common Regulatory Régime?

There are two contentious issues in taxi regulation. First, should there be any distinction between taxis and hire cars? Second, at what level of government should regulation be placed? Failure to decide these matters underlies the weakness of existing regulation.

It is difficult to justify separate régimes for taxis and hire cars, since each provides essentially the same service. Provided standards of quality are maintained, there is no reason why differences in regulation should continue. Furthermore, if these standards are to be nationally applicable, there is no need for separate local licensing authorities.

Instead, there is a regulatory régime already in existence into which they could be brought. With some modification, the Operator's Licence required for buses and lorries could well extend to both taxi and hire cars, treated as a single mode of transport. The principal adjustment would be the need to provide for the owner-driver. Vehicles thus authorised, by the Regional Traffic Commissioners, would be able to ply for hire anywhere, whether by pre-booking, by standing on a rank, or by cruising.

Apart from ensuring an open market for the combined trade, two further advantages would flow from such a régime. *First*, it would no longer be necessary for a cab that has taken a fare to a point outside its licensed area to return empty.[22] There is no reason why a cab should be treated as just a short-journey mode of transport; local authority boundaries have little to do with catchment areas for traffic.

[22] Birmingham International Airport, the International Station and the National Exhibition Centre lie in Solihull Borough, and Birmingham taxis can only be used to carry return loads from them if they have a second licence from Solihull.

The *second* advantage of a unified régime, with no quantity control, is in economic efficiency and innovation. In New York, the number of cabs has been kept the same since 1937, so that by 1990 the cost of a licence to trade was around $125,000[23]—which must be recouped from customers. In a reasonably contestable market, on the other hand, the entry price is little more than the cost of the vehicle: the pressure of competition will lead firms and drivers to seek new ways of gaining revenue. We have already seen how the development of taxibuses in Britain is set around by complex regulations,[24] put in place, no doubt, to placate the vested interest of the bus industry. A good example of what could be possible is the system of 'fixed-route' taxis, observed by the present author in the Chilean capital, Santiago, in 1981.[25] From ranks in the city centre, cabs leave for specific sectors of the suburbs, the first on the rank leaving when full, and taking its passengers to their doors. Inward journeys would be pre-booked, but again the driver would do a sort of mental linear programming exercise to determine his optimal route. Fares were about five times the equivalent by bus. Such schemes as this, midway between the traditional taxi and the urban minibus, show how a liberalised transport system can serve to make the taxi 'just another form of transport'.

What Can Railways Contribute?

The phrasing of this question is important. If we are to address the market for mobility, we must not ask 'what can *British Rail* contribute?' There is a new confidence in the future viability of railway transport throughout Europe and America. That is to be welcomed, but there are still problems associated with what Professor Gourvish has called 'the culture of the rail'.[26] This paper will not concern itself with the current controversies about privatisation, save in so far as they follow from the contribution of rail transport to mobility.

As Table 3 shows, railways today are a minority carrier,

[23] See 'All the world's a cab', *The Economist*, 22 December 1990.

[24] See above, page 27.

[25] See J. Hibbs, *Regulation: An international study of bus and coach licensing*, Tregaron, Dyfed: Brefi Press, 1985.

[26] T.R. Gourvish, *British Railways 1948-1973, A Business History*, Cambridge: Cambridge University Press, 1986.

whether of passengers or goods, the percentage of passenger traffic having fallen by more than half from an already low figure since 1955.[27] What is more, since the data consist of passenger kilometres, and rail trips tend to be longer on average than those for other modes of transport (air travel apart), the proportion of *people* involved must be even lower. Only in the special circumstances of London commuting, where over 75 per cent of passengers in 1990 travelled by rail,[28] does the train come into its own as a mass provider of mobility.

Despite this, railway transport is treated as a special case. For one thing, it is heavily subsidised; in 1990/91 19 per cent of British Rail's total revenue came from public sources.[29] But

TABLE 3

THE SHIFT FROM RAIL TO ROAD: GREAT BRITAIN, 1955-1990

(Percentages)

Year	Passengers		Freight			
	Passenger kms		Tonnes lifted		Tonne kms	
	Road	Rail	Road	Rail	Road	Rail
1955	82	18	75	21	41	38
1960	84	16	80	17	49	30
1965	89	10	83	12	58	21
1970	90	9	84	11	63	18
1975	91	8	85	10	66	15
1980	92	7	79	9	53	10
1985	93	7	80	7	55	8
1990	93	6	81	7	62	7

Notes: Basis of freight calculation changed in 1976.
Figures do not sum to 100 because of other modes (air, sea, inland waterway, pipeline).

Source: *Transport Statistics Great Britain 1991*, London: HMSO, 1991, Tables 1.1, 7.1; 1.13, 7.3.

[27] *Transport Statistics Great Britain 1992, op. cit.* The comparable figures for freight movement (in tonne-kilometres) are 42 per cent in 1952 and 7 per cent in 1991.

[28] *Transport Statistics Great Britain 1991*, London: HMSO, 1991.

[29] *Ibid.*

the political implications of subsidisation have been hardly recognised, despite their analysis in a book which has been strangely neglected since its appearance in 1975.[30] Having examined the use of railway services by income group, the authors concluded that 50 per cent of personal expenditure on rail travel was accounted for by the top 20 per cent of households, despite the fact that they accounted for only a third of all expenditure. They pointed out that the highest income groups must also have accounted for the great bulk of business expenditure on rail travel, despite the fact that their share of all expenditure was around 8 per cent.

This led them to conclude that extra taxation to meet the cost of railway subsidy would be regressive, given the nature of UK fiscal policies, and that the existing subsidy policy must 'contribute to inequality'. There seems little reason to suppose that the regressive effect of the railway subsidy has markedly changed since they wrote.

For the railway to play its part in the market for mobility, the clouds of nostalgia must be blown away to enable it to be seen, like the car and the taxi, as 'just another form of transport'. From their contemporary low base, and freed from decades of government nannying, the potential contribution of railways could be surprising. In the USA, freight railways given up for dead have returned to profitability since the Staggers Act swept away outdated controls in 1980.[31]

Despite the progressive dismantling of controls in Britain since 1953, the railways have not shown the same resilience, probably because they have remained dependent upon government as a source of funds for expansion, and to a large extent for re-equipment. Such funds as have been made available have not always been well spent,[32] but the conclusion is inescapable that both British Rail and London Underground operations have been severely distorted since 1947 by political interference in their investment and pricing policies. One sensible reform, now promised, would be to place investment criteria for highway and railway schemes on an even footing; for far too long the basis for calculating the

[30] R.W.S. Pryke & J.S. Dodgson, *The Rail Problem*, London: Martin Robertson, 1975: see Ch.9, 'The Social Benefits of Rail Passenger Services'.

[31] See Albro Martin, *Railroads Triumphant*, Oxford: Oxford University Press, 1992.

[32] See Gourvish, *op. cit.*

return on motorway building has been a form of cost-benefit analysis, incorporating externalities, while spending on railways has required a financial rate of return not including external effects. The problems associated with the construction of the Channel Tunnel rail links have no doubt influenced the Government's belated attention to the issue, but until both rail and highway ownership are firmly in the private sector[33] the danger of political interference, and the straitjacket of the public sector borrowing requirement (PSBR), will remain.

The provision of 'socially necessary' train services, currently achieved by way of a block grant for the 'public service obligation', raises issues best treated along with those associated with the bus industry.[34] But the serious problems of London commuting are not part of the same issue, since they arise from misguided charging policies over some 25 years, which have made public transport in the capital cheaper than its finances justify. The distortions in land-use and settlement patterns that have followed from vote-seeking policies at the cost of economic efficiency will not be rectified by more of the same.

Paternalism and the Tram

Trams, like trains, are a ripe field for nostalgia. The sole remaining full-scale line, at Blackpool, is a significant tourist attraction. Crowds go to ride on old tramcars at the Crich Tramway Museum in Derbyshire, who would not thank the authorities if they had to use one to get to work. There is also an element of nostalgia in the current fashion, among local authorities if not among their taxpayers, for the resurgence of the electric tram in the form of Light Rapid Transit (LRT).[35]

In Continental cities, including many which had to re-equip after 1945, modern tramcars were introduced, and there has been a continued development of the mode. This reflects in part greater population density, where more people live in flats than is usual in Britain, but it also follows from a cultural

---

[33] See J. Hibbs and G. Roth, *Tomorrow's Way: Managing roads in a free society*, London: Adam Smith Institute, 1992.

[34] See below, page 85.

[35] The present author claims to have been the first to denominate the letters 'LRT' as meaning 'Love Running Trams'.

difference that allows central planning to use a substantial element of subsidy in providing for urban mobility. The same approach is to be seen in the United States, and one of its consequences has been the use of Light Rapid Transit as a term that avoids the dated (and down-market) image of the tram.

Promotion of LRT in recent years in Britain has reflected the loss of control of public transport by local authority planners as a consequence of reforms by the late (Lord) Nicholas Ridley. Substantial sums of public money have been spent on feasibility studies, some with an air of fantasy about them. While councillors have enjoyed visits to Lille and Grenoble at the taxpayer's expense, to see the latest technology, the reluctance of government to provide the large capital sums required to build a system reflects not only current financial stringency but also a perception that LRT is too often a solution looking for a problem.

No pure LRT system has yet been built in the UK. The Tyneside Metro replaced a life-expired railway, and the new Manchester line has done the same, but with a stretch of street tramway. In Ireland, the DART[36] is a suburban railway misnamed. But the real point at issue, against which further schemes must be tested, is the method of financial appraisal. Until it can be shown that methods of appraisal are consistent with those used for investment in roads and railways, it will be uncertain whether public funds are being employed in ways which reflect their opportunity cost.

Whether LRT should be promoted as a means of dealing with street congestion is doubtful in the absence of road-use pricing.[37] There may be a case for investment in an alternative infrastructure, where the concentration of demand warrants it. But that should not encourage LRT development as a paternalistic means of supplying what planners think people want, while running a transport business in competition with commercial operators who have a bottom line to consider which the planners lack.

Low-Tech Transit

One serious disadvantage of almost every LRT scheme so far proposed is the need for a substantial number of its passengers

---

[36] Dublin Area Rapid Transit.

[37] See below, Section IV.

to travel by another mode to use it, thus raising penalties in terms of generalised cost which are seldom taken into account. By setting out to distance LRT from the traditional tram, its proponents open themselves to the criticism that they have re-invented the wheel.[38] Yet so often they claim that investment in LRT can be justified only if bus services are re-routed to direct people on to the new system, whether or not that is what they would prefer.

The undoubted attraction of LRT, on the other hand, is its superiority over other modes in the economical use of land. The 'track discipline' of railborne transport enables traffic to flow in large quantities (provided always there is sufficient demand) without the congestion that arises on the roads. Point-to-point speeds are therefore higher, although the 'lapsed time' from start to finish of each passenger's trip may not be so markedly improved. Its advantage lies in its ability, where land is available, to by-pass inner-city areas, where streets are narrow and traffic at its heaviest. Whether it links the city to wealthy suburbs or to peripheral housing estates, LRT can be made to sound a very attractive proposition.

It is, however, expensive, and subject to lengthy statutory processes before construction can begin.[39] If siting has been misjudged, it quickly becomes a notorious white elephant. And if it is financed out of taxation, then those with homes in the poorer areas of the inner city will be contributing to an investment from which they will have little to gain. Moreover, it is likely to weaken the competitive position of the bus, by siphoning off investment that could have improved the highway, and by its competitive advantage achieved, in almost every case so far proposed, because of public funding.

Advantages of 'Busways' over LRT

There is an alternative which, while lacking the high-tech glamour of LRT, offers all its advantages.[40] This is something

[38] The designers of the Bay Area Rapid Transit System (BART) at San Francisco made the memorable announcement that they had developed an entirely new form of transport—the duorail!

[39] The delay has now been reduced by the new procedures introduced by the Transport and Works Act 1992.

[40] The environmental gains associated with electric traction that are often claimed in support of LRT must be set against the CO_2 emissions from power stations which it must substantially increase.

usually called a *busway*—a system, or just a stretch of road, available for the use of buses only. Its success in Runcorn in Cheshire, where it has been built as an alternative to LRT, has gone largely unnoticed, but more recently it has been developed in several countries to form a distinct mode of transport, which can be called KGB (or 'kerb-guided buses')— described and discussed in more detail in Box 1 (below, pp.36-37).

Unlike LRT, the KGB system can be open for any operator to use whose vehicles are fitted with the necessary device. It offers all the benefits of LRT in terms of track discipline, and betters them both as to economy in the use of land, and the minimisation of lapsed time for the overall trip. Unlike LRT, KGB obviates the need to change vehicles, since the buses can 'fan out' to serve the lower density housing at the outer end of the route.[41] The construction of KGB tracks could be funded from the surplus arising from road-use pricing (Section IV), or even, where topography permits, by private investment in the necessary land.

Assuming the objective is a harmonised régime for the various modes of providing mobility, the disadvantages of LRT (with its tendency to regressive taxation and its atavistic overtones of tramway-style paternalism) can be avoided by the use of KGB, which also makes the best of the traditional motor bus.

Back to the Bus?

The Victorian artist Alfred Morgan painted a picture called *An omnibus ride to Piccadilly Circus: Mr Gladstone travelling with ordinary passengers*. It shows the 'Grand Old Man', as he was affectionately known, in the company of people who would have been 'of the better class'. Today it is news if a Cabinet Minister uses public transport (other than InterCity trains), but it is Mr Gladstone's travelling companions who emphasise the change that has taken place. Their equivalent 100 years later would be unlikely to ride in an omnibus (although 40 years ago they still might have done).

---

[41] A variant currently being proposed in Bristol and Portsmouth by the Badgerline group of companies would use a dual mode vehicle, powered by a diesel engine in the suburbs, but drawing current from a wire in the way a trolleybus does in sections where it would be guided by a wheel bearing in a slot in a busway. This is called GLT—Guided Light Transit.

BOX 1

'KGB', or Priority for the Bus

The letters 'KGB' have changed their connotation. They now stand for a method of liberating the bus from the chains of street congestion by a technique called *kerb-guided buses.* A concrete track, wide enough for a bus, and with a high kerb, is built where congestion is a problem, and the necessary land is available. Buses are fitted with a device which consists of a small horizontal wheel, which bears on the kerb and guides the bus, relieving the driver of the necessity to steer. At the end of this busway, services can 'fan out' into housing areas in a way that would be impracticable for railed vehicles.

Access to the busway is through a 'gate'. A short section has two separate tracks, such that the wheels of the bus fit into them, and between them there is a set of blocks or spikes which will prevent cars, with their narrower track, passing through. Similar gates are placed at any intersections along the busway, and at its end.

KGB has several important advantages over LRT (light rapid transit). One has already been mentioned*—the ability of the buses to serve areas where the high cost of LRT (or the traditional trolleybus) would be prohibitive. Another is the greatly reduced 'landtake' required for its construction: whereas LRT requires two tracks, the busway requires only a single track which is used on a 'tidal flow' basis - in the direction of the peak traffic - since buses coming in the opposite direction can use the relatively

*Above, p. 35.

The decline in social status of the bus in Britain has not been matched in some other West European and Scandinavian countries, at least for urban mobility. True, people have not always been given the same freedom to choose their preferred mode as they have in Britain, France and Italy, where urban car use is relatively high. But it is also true that public transport in Continental European cities has been retained at a high standard by substantial subsidy, while the British bus industry, even when in receipt of subsidy, has been marked by increasingly down-market status.

[36]

empty carriageway on the other side. Then there is the greatly reduced cost of a concrete track compared with the provision of steel rails, points and crossing. KGB obviates the necessity for the heavy expenditure on vehicles, depots and maintenance equipment which LRT requires, because the buses and their garages are there already.

But it is for the consumer and the economy that 'KGB' shows its very real advantage, inasmuch as it need not interfere with competition. Any firm prepared to fit the controlling device may use the busway; firms that do not want to do so can still use the ordinary carriageway. That it is a workable system has been shown in Australia and Germany, as well as on a stretch of suburban road in Birmingham (where there was no congestion to justify it). The place for a busway is along the median strip of a dual carriageway, or through an inner-city area where space permits. It can be built with minimum formality, as a result of the Transport and Works Act 1992, and, because it is used by diesel buses, it avoids the CO_2 pollution involved in any form of electric traction, such as Light Rapid Transit.

A KGB busway is now being constructed in Leeds, where the Yorkshire Rider bus company is an advocate of the system. A variant has been proposed for Bristol and Portsmouth by the Badgerline group—this one would use a dual mode vehicle, powered by a light diesel engine in the suburbs, or on the open carriageway, but drawing current from a wire in the way a trolleybus does in sections where it would be guided by a wheel bearing in a slot in the busway. This variant is called 'GLT'— guided light transit.

In Britain, the transport industry generally has a poor image and its management is hardly recognised as offering a rewarding career. Bus travel in particular declined because the industry for so long attracted neither entrepreneurial flair nor high and reliable levels of subsidy. Lacking status and reward, managers watched their customers desert the buses for their preferred choice, the private car. Moreover, cocooned in the protectionist licensing system, they failed to make a serious attempt to halt the decline of their market share.[42]

[42] It is a sad reflection that, until very recently, bus managers did not use terms like market share.

After three decades of quantity control had stifled entrepreneurship, subsidy when it came was applied to an already declining mode of travel. The product of the industry then came to be seen as a commodity of last resort, and its organisation began to form part of the welfare state. Buses continued to run on invisible tramlines; subsidy gave union negotiators the edge over managers, leading to wage drift; and not only was customer care unheard of, but the idea that there might be new customers to attract had become foreign to the culture of the bus.

The Resurgence of Management

Despite the criticism of regulatory reform and privatisation that has come from the Association of Metropolitan Authorities (AMA), and the pressure for outworn centralising policies which emanates from some professional organisations,[43] managers in the bus industry have no wish to go down the franchise route proposed by the Labour and Liberal Democrat parties in their 1992 General Election manifestoes, and recommended again recently in some newspapers.[44] The Bus and Coach Council, speaking as the industry's trade association, has accepted the post-1985 régime, and mounted a successful promotional campaign, 'Buses Mean Business'. Addressing the senior enthusiast society, the Chairman of a former state-owned bus company said: 'I believe that in many ways deregulation will be the industry's saviour'.[45] He went on to emphasise the need for quality legislation as well as for some rethinking in the Office of Fair Trading, and endorsed the Bus and Coach Council's promotional manifesto, *Putting Passengers First.*

Independent studies of the industry show how it is emerging from the shadows of political control and finding its feet in a commercial environment, at a time when the state of the nation's economy is hardly propitious. Significantly, far more is now known about the industry's performance than in the years of public ownership. The viability of many companies remains

[43] See below, page 77.

[44] See, for example, the leading article, 'A better way for buses', in the *Financial Times*, 15 June 1992, which echoed the reactionary views of the AMA.

[45] Brian King, Presidential Address to the Omnibus Society, reproduced in *The Omnibus Magazine*, April/May 1992.

questionable, the overall profit margin (1·5 per cent in 1990/91) being insufficient for firms in many places to replace their assets[46] (though performance varied widely from a profit of 19·4 per cent to a loss of 23·2 per cent). Current problems apart, the economic prospects for the bus industry appear good. In the words of a recent report:

'Congestion and environmental concerns have already begun to turn the tide against car usage. This and the increasing likelihood of a more constructive and co-ordinated Governmental approach to transport planning, could provide the bus and coach industry with an opportunity to turn its own tide of fortunes for the better.'[47]

Firms that survive the recession, this implies, should face a bright future, provided always that managers are able to take advantage of better times to come; and that the Government's planning does not undermine the benefits of the market.

There is every reason to expect them to do so. The competence of management in the bus industry is impressive, owing not a little to the senior management training scheme of the erstwhile National Bus Company, which advanced the careers of 180 people, many of them in chief executive posts in bus companies today.[48] Although the rejuvenation of bus management has not been accompanied by any significant influx of new blood, it is encouraging that so much advantage has been taken of the new freedom to manage autonomously in an open market.[49] Innovations over the past eight years[50] show what progress was waiting to be made.

---

[46] Figures quoted here are from the *Bus Industry Monitor 1992*, Preston: Transport Advisory Service, 1992.

[47] M.O.W. Hastings and E.R. Thompson, *The UK Bus and Coach Sector: Total business and political environment*, London: Management & Marketing Strategy Analysts, 1991.

[48] See J.A. Birks *et al.*, *National Bus Company 1968-1989, A Commemorative Volume*, Glossop: Transport Publishing Company, 1990, pp.539-43.

[49] Concern must be expressed lest the next generation of managers suffers from the absence of any successor to the training scheme.

[50] See Section III.

III. THE BUS IN THE MARKET

Mr Ridley's Mine

The previously highly competitive bus and coach industry was transformed by the Road Traffic Act 1930 into a closely regulated system of route monopolists, subject to price control which after 1950 was enforced on the basis of a standard rate per mile, irrespective of market conditions. There were three sectors: the large 'territorial' companies, in which the railways invested in the 1930s; the municipal undertakings; and the 'independents' (mainly small firms, but including a few larger ones). Only the charter side of the business was unregulated though quality control extended to every kind of operator.

The Transport Act of 1968 completed the nationalisation of the territorial companies and established Passenger Transport Authorities (PTAs) in four of the English conurbations, which inherited the municipal fleets in their areas and were given powers of compulsory purchase and duties of co-ordination. A Greater Glasgow (later Strathclyde) authority followed, and the Local Government Act of 1972 made the new Metropolitan Councils PTAs, thereby extending their boundaries and creating two new ones. The 1968 Act also gave the 'shire' councils powers and duties of co-ordination, so that the remaining element of managerial autonomy was virtually stifled.

The Local Government Act also provided for increased subsidy to bus operation, following the conclusions of a parliamentary committee,[1] which had argued that such subsidies, by improving the quality of bus services, would reduce the need for massive road investment. That proved to be incorrect but the subsidy powers were widely used for social and political ends by the new Metropolitan Councils.

Operations in the metropolitan counties became the responsibility of Passenger Transport Executives, whose commercial freedom was constrained by the oversight of the District Auditor. Elsewhere the state-owned National Bus Company and Scottish Bus Group, while working through

[1] See *Report of the Expenditure Committee on Urban Transport Planning*, HC Paper 57-I, Session 1972-73, London: HMSO, 1973.

[41]

wholly-owned subsidiary companies, gave little commercial freedom to their managers. In London, where public transport had always tended to be given special treatment, the whole post-war period was marked by vote-seeking intervention in the management of the clumsy and over-large bus undertaking, with predictable consequences for efficiency and customer satisfaction.[2]

In total, the consequence of these policies was to put council bureaucrats and their political masters in the place of consumers as the 'customers' of the bus industry. There was now no 'bottom line', but instead there was growing frustration for professional managers whose decision-making powers were being taken from them into the shadow world of 'co-ordination'. The consequences for economic efficiency were predictable: the White Paper *Buses* reported that between 1972 and 1982, operating costs rose by between 15 per cent and 30 per cent more than the rate of inflation, much of this being due to wage (and salary) 'drift', as union representatives exploited the weaknesses that follow from large-scale subsidy. The increase in costs was the more remarkable in that the period saw the decimation of the previous force of bus conductors, as the 'new bus grant', designed to convert fleets to rear-engined vehicles, made buses suitable for driver-only operation. Expected savings seem to have been more than offset by mechanical problems with the early rear-engine designs.

Rapid Rise in State Subsidy, 1972-82

The decade also saw an increase in revenue support that must have sounded warning bells in the Treasury, as the sums involved rose from £10 million in 1972 to £520 million 10 years later; even in real terms the increase was 13 times. The greater part went to monopolistic, publicly owned operators in London, the metropolitan counties, and Strathclyde. Increases stemmed mainly from product-driven management, as the need to satisfy the customer (as passenger) faded into the background. In pursuit of increased labour productivity, larger buses were operated less frequently, despite the

---

[2] For London, see P.E. Garbutt, *London Transport and the Politicians*, Shepperton, Middlesex: Ian Allan, 1985, and for the story in England and Wales, see J.A. Birks *et al.*, *National Bus Company 1968-1989, A Commemorative Volume*, Glossop: Transport Publishing Company, 1990. A study of the Scottish experience in the period is still awaited.

evidence then available that passengers do not like waiting at bus stops. Standards of comfort and of customer care fell, and the political decision in some councils to hold down fares (or even, in South Yorkshire, to do away with them) merely worsened the operating deficit, which then had to be made up at the expense of road maintenance, or loaded onto the local rates.

Even more remarkable was the failure of the industry to promote its own product, shown by the weakness of its publicity effort, criticised in two contemporary reports.[3] Having failed since 1950 to respond to the growing competition of the private car—perhaps having failed at first even to recognise it—the bus industry by the end of the 1970s was suffering from the debilitating effects of statutory protection, re-inforced (not least in the great cities) by the similar consequences of subsidy. The situation could not be allowed to continue, as politicians on both sides of the House were beginning to recognise. After some tinkering in the Transport Act 1980 (including the removal of price control), the whole structure of regulation and subsidy was blown up by the late Nicholas Ridley's Act of 1985, returning the bus industry to the market—yet with significant reservations.

In 1984 the Government published a White Paper with the simple title of *Buses*,[4] which reflected the argument of a series of *Hobart Papers*.[5] As it became plain that there was to be no negotiation with the industry, there was an outbreak of fury which made the ensuing political argument peculiarly bitter. For there is a market for regulation, as for anything that people value, and it had been assumed that bargains had been struck in the form of the Acts of 1930 and 1968. These bargains, it was plain, were now to be unilaterally denounced through the high-handedness (not to mention high-mindedness) of the Secretary of State.

---

[3] J. Cartledge, *See How They Run: The Design of Passenger Information Literature*, London: London Transport Passengers Committee, 1984 (but not limited to London), and *Catching up with the bus*, London: National Consumer Council, 1985.

[4] Cmnd.9300, London: HMSO, 1984.

[5] No.23, *Transport for Passengers*, by the present author (1963, revised 2nd edition, 1971); No.49, *Transport Policy: Co-ordination through Competition*, by the late G.J. Ponsonby (1969); and No.95, *Transport Without Politics...?*, again by the present author (1982). The White Paper reflected a number of the arguments of Hobart Paper 95, except for the recommendation for road-use pricing as a *sine qua non* for bus deregulation.

Transport Act 1985

The objectives of the Transport Act 1985 may be listed as follows:

○ to force a supply-driven industry to become market-led, by repealing the protectionist legislation of 1930;
○ to privatise the subsidiary companies of the National Bus Company and the Scottish Bus Group;
○ to move the municipal bus undertakings (including those of the metropolitan county councils) nearer to commercial freedom by turning them into wholly-owned companies;
○ to provide for a transparent and much reduced subsidy for 'socially necessary' bus services;
○ to force managers to become more commercial by withdrawing all supply-side ('network') subsidy, and forbidding cross-subsidisation of loss-making services;
○ to erect residual defences of 'the public interest' by repealing the industry's exemption from the fair trading laws;
○ to encourage new entry to the trade and consumer-oriented innovation.

With political caution the Act was not to apply to London, where instead a régime of controlled franchise was to be progressively established in order to encourage new entry and to reduce supply-side subsidy. Introduction of the changes was arranged on a step-by-step basis, whereby the new regulatory system would not become fully effective until 26 January 1987. Privatisation, however, was to commence from the passage of the Act, and the commercialisation of the municipal undertakings was to take effect from 26 October 1986, the date when the 1930 licensing system was to expire. A complicating factor was the abolition of the metropolitan county councils on 1 April 1986, which necessitated the creation of *ad hoc* organisations to inherit certain of their powers, which were, ironically, the Passenger Transport Authorities of the 1968 Transport Act.

The reaction of the bus industry was confused. While a highly vocal and well-organised opposition to the Bill was mounted by the establishment, supported by a selection of politicians from all parties, a new and very capable generation of younger managers welcomed the prospect of freedom from the nannying of local authorities, whose preoccupation with minor issues had often diverted attention from the effective operation of the main revenue-earning bus routes. Many of these managers worked in state-owned companies about to be privatised, but others were in the municipal sector, and could see the opportunities for improvement which would open up when they were free from the council committee's day-to-day control. Very little enthusiasm for the Bill came from the 'independent' sector of small family firms, which recognised the value of the route licence which had protected them for so long from competition. The present author was made aware of one private firm which in 1975 had turned down an offer of £250,000 for the goodwill of a licensed express coach service, only to find that after 1980 it would hardly be worth a tenth of that sum.

But there was much opposition to the Bill, some of it carried to a melodramatic and ludicrous extent. Not a few county council officers and senior bus company managers ought to have been embarrassed by the failure of subsequent events to measure up to their prognostications. There were 'ancestral voices, prophesying war', and the opposition rallied to its cause trade unions and that whole class of intellectuals and academics criticised by Hayek for its contempt for and ignorance of economics. (Transport departments in universities and polytechnics, almost always to be found in faculties of engineering or planning, were with few exceptions opposed to the Bill, as were the majority of amateurs of the industry.) Public meetings were held, dominated by emotion rather than rational argument.

The British bus industry at the time of the Ridley Bill had become very much of a channel for supporting the assumed mobility 'needs' of the poor. Despite the considerable (and increasing) flow of funds from taxation, it was not doing a very good job, as has been witnessed by the improved access to homes since the opportunity for innovation was restored in 1986.[6] The legacy of 50 years of protectionism, combined with the nannying of councillors and council officers, who had replaced passengers as the customers of the industry, meant that bus operators were not highly regarded. Mr Ridley's mine, as it exploded, cleared the landscape of much that belonged to an irrelevant past. The new generation has taken advantage of the liberty that ensued to set about the

---

[6] See the present author's article, 'An Evaluation of Urban Bus Deregulation in Britain: A Survey of Management Attitudes', *Progress in Planning*, Vol.36, 1991.

business of satisfying effective demand in place of the edicts of local authorities, and seems to be making an enjoyable living out of doing it.

The Outcome of Reform

Inevitably the media dubbed 26 October 1986, the day the bus industry was supposed to be deregulated, D-Day, or 'the big bang', despite the fact that another three months were to pass before the final stage of deregulation was reached. It was suggested that buses were to pass from 'BC' (Before Competition) to 'AD' (After Deregulation).[7] But in practice D-Day was a Sunday, so the planned changes made themselves felt chiefly on Monday the 27th.

Over much of the country even this was a non-event. The state-owned and private sector companies had taken advantage of the easing of route licensing by the 1980 Transport Act to make any necessary changes in advance; as Table 4 shows, they had less to lose from the ending of supply-side subsidy, and they had had fully 12 months from the passage of the 1985 Act in which to make their plans. In the Potteries, for example, the company's post-deregulation pattern of services was in place by the end of June 1986.

For the most part it was in the former metropolitan counties that people experienced deregulation as chaos on the streets, though even these varied. In nearly every case there was a major restructuring that took effect on the morning of 27 October. Not surprisingly, given the weakness of the industry's publicity effort, many people were faced that day with confusion and inadequate or misleading information. In those conurbations with some form of local train service the immediate beneficiary was British Rail.

The degree of competition which appeared after deregulation varied widely. Some commentators then criticised the new régime for creating instability, while others condemned it as a failure because competition had not broken out. One effect of the new contestability[8] was to

---

[7] I am indebted to my colleague Mr Ian Dickins for this formulation.

[8] Contestability is a relatively recent term for a familiar concept: the extent to which a market is open to new or increased competition: see W.J. Baumol, 'Contestable Markets', *American Economic Review*, Vol.72, 1982, pp.1-15. Deregulation has not of course produced fully contestable markets; apart from the remaining elements of control (see below), there remains an element of sunk cost in setting up a bus business, which acts as a barrier to entry.

TABLE 4

SOURCES OF REVENUE FOR BUS OPERATORS: GREAT BRITAIN, 1982/83

(Percentages)

Origins of revenue	Type of operator				
	LTE BUS	*PTE*	*NBC/SBG*	*MUNICIPAL*	*ALL PUBLIC OPERATORS*
Passenger and other receipts [1]	46	55	76	65	62
Concessionary fares payments	11	13	7	14	10
Revenue support	44[2]	32	17[3]	21	28
TOTAL	100	100	100	100	100

Notes: [1] 'Other' receipts are from advertising, carriage of parcels, etc.
            [2] Includes depreciation and renewal grants.
            [3] Includes reimbursement of expenses under operating agency agreements.

Rebate of fuel duty is omitted, as applicable equally to private sector firms.

LTE - London Transport Executive
PTE - Passenger Transport Executives
NBC - National Bus Company
SBG - Scottish Bus Group

Source: White Paper, *Buses,* Cmnd. 9300, London: HMSO, 1984.

increase the effectiveness of many already market-dominant firms. There may be differing cultural attitudes between small firms in different cities so that some are more ready than others to try their hands at running bus services. The success or failure of the policy outlined in *Buses* should not be judged by the extent of competition on the streets, for it is the threat of entry rather than actual confrontation that ensures the benefits of the market process. At Bristol, for example, capable management of the privatised company delivered substantial improvements to the bus services, resulting in increased carryings, in a city where very little competition actually appeared.

The district, county and (in Scotland) regional bus undertakings now became Public Transport Companies (PTCs), and their performance seems to have varied according to the degree of autonomy allowed to their managers by their municipal shareholders. One or two smaller ones have failed to survive. In Greater Manchester and on Mersyside the incumbent PTCs were faced with substantial competition, both from newly privatised firms and from small businesses, some set up by staff made redundant by the PTC itself. In both conurbations the Passenger Transport Authority established interventionist policies for the management of their PTCs, which did not improve their prospects of solvency. The Greater Manchester company was instructed to be 'non-profit-making', while on Merseyside the bus companies were faced with 'socially necessary' services, provided under contract at fares lower than their own. During 1991 new chief executives were appointed to each of these PTCs, with the responsibility of establishing their financial health; the Merseyside company has since been sold to its staff, for a nominal price, while the Government is forcing the break-up and sale of the PTC in Greater Manchester, after dogged political resistance.

The PTCs in Tyne & Wear and West Yorkshire, which were sold to their management and staff early in the period, have proved to be successful and innovative. The South Yorkshire PTC, having overcome the problems of returning to a normal pricing régime and also facing severe on-the-road competition, has proved its command of marketing management, in an industry where its importance is not always recognised. Marketing skills have enabled a number of newcomers to establish themselves, some of which have since succumbed to what seems close to predatory behaviour on the part of larger neighbours, and some others have thought it wise to accept an offer for their business 'that they could not afford to refuse'. Widespread competition from and between small firms in South Wales brought consumers a wider choice than they had known for many years, and undoubtedly expanded the market; one former NBC company there weathered the storm, but another has been unable to survive. Overall, a healthy range of management styles and initiatives has succeeded the centralisation that was characteristic of the National Bus Company, and the politicisation of the municipal sector.

Deregulation and Competition Policy

It would be mistaken to assume, as some have done, that the consequences of the Ridley explosion have been catastrophic. On 11 February 1987, a few weeks into full deregulation, the newspaper *Bus Business* asked in its leader 'What became of the dereg disaster?'. Table 5 illustrates the way output (measured by the increase in vehicle kilometres travelled) increased, with sales continuing their secular downward trend, but the figures mask the instances where managers of newly privatised companies used their freedom from both route licensing and the National Bus Company to hold their own, and even increase carryings, in one case by as much as 26 per cent. Table 6 shows the effect on prices and highlights the special case of the former metropolitan counties, where supply-side subsidy had been used to hold fares down. In South Yorkshire the council's policy had been to phase out fares altogether, and there was an increase of 225 per cent. These figures, made much of by the (socialist) Association of Metropolitan Authorities, must be set against the ability of the bus industry outside London and the metropolitan areas to keep fare increases in line with the retail price index.

The most extensive study of the consequences of the 1985 Transport Act[9] certainly does not support the idea that they have been disastrous, but since it was limited to the former metropolitan counties it neglects the experience of the rest

[9] L. Pickup *et al.*, *Bus Deregulation in Metropolitan Areas*, Aldershot: Avebury (Oxford Studies in Transport Series), 1991.

TABLE 5

BUS AND COACH OPERATORS' OUTPUT AND SALES: GREAT BRITAIN, 1982-1991

(Local (stage) services)

Output - Million vehicle kilometres
Sales - Million passenger journeys

Area and measure	Period									
	1982	1983	1984	1985	1986	1987	1988/89	1989/90	1990/91	

All outside London

	1982	1983	1984	1985	1986	1987	1988/89	1989/90	1990/91
Output	1,846	1,853	1,857	1,803	1,881	2,065	2,103	2,152	2,140
Sales	4,477	4,500	4,488	4,489	4,160	4,071	3,995	3,874	3,654

All outside London and English Metropolitan Counties

	1982	1983	1984	1985	1986	1987	1988/89	1989/90	1990/91
Output	1,261	1,271	1,273	1,228	1,323	1,447	1,470	1,500	1,491
Sales	2,496	2,489	2,441	2,420	2,349	2,338	2,300	2,232	2,126

All Great Britain

	1982	1983	1984	1985	1986	1987	1988/89	1989/90	1990/91
Output	2,111	2,117	2,125	2,076	2,159	2,341	2,389	2,445	2,444
Sales	5,518	5,587	5,650	5,641	5,325	5,311	5,236	5,085	4,851

Notes: Estimates by area for 1982 to 1984 are derived from a number of sources and may be less reliable than those for later years.

Source: Transport Statistics Great Britain 1992. London: HMSO. 1992. Tables 5.1 and 5.2.

[50]

TABLE 6
BUS FARES: INDICES BY AREA, GREAT BRITAIN, 1982-1991
(1985 = 100)
(Local (stage) services)

Year	London	English Metropolitan Areas	England	Area Scotland	Great Britain	All outside London	All non-met.*	Retail prices index
1982	98·1	97·6	89·4	89·1	88·7	87·7	84·1	85·9
1983	100·0	99·5	94·2	94·6	93·8	92·8	90·3	89·8
1984	91·6	98·6	95·3	98·4	95·8	96·6	95·8	94·3
1985/6	101·7	100·4	101·1	100·2	100·9	100·8	101·0	101·2
1986/7	107·8	129·3	112·7	103·7	111·1	111·7	105·7	104·4
1987/8	113·1	140·0	119·5	107·8	117·4	118·3	110·7	108·6
1988/9	125·3	148·9	127·3	112·2	124·6	124·5	116·2	115·1
1989/90	138·2	161·2	138·1	117·9	134·5	133·9	124·9	124·1
1990/91	152·4	176·4	152·1	126·9	147·8	147·0	136·9	136·1

Note: *All outside London and English Metropolitan Areas.
Source: Transport Statistics Great Britain 1992, London: HMSO, 1992, Table 5.6.

of the country (which includes a number of significant conurbations). The passage of time makes it increasingly difficult to compare the old and new dispensations, but in any case there is no comprehensive study which reports the notable success stories as well as recording the inevitable weaknesses. The extent of competition has, however, been studied,[10] and the conclusions reported are worth noting:

o The rate of incidence of new on-the-road competition declined from a peak following deregulation to a small but significant level by September 1990. By this time most of the new competition was being initiated by small operators.

o Over half (398 out of 762) of the cases of competition which started before September 1990 were still active by the end of that month.

o Competition has most often taken the form of small operators encroaching on the 'territories' of larger established operators.

o Where competition comes to an end, the larger operator is more likely to survive, even in the minority of cases where the smaller operator has 'home advantage'.

The authors remark, cautiously, that

'A dynamic state of equilibrium seems to have been established, with new cases of competition replacing those which come to an end' (p.19).

The policy was not one of 'total deregulation'. The new régime left in place EC regulations which require a valid Operator's Licence to be held if bus or coach services, including private charter, are to be offered 'for hire or reward'. The licence, which states the number of vehicles authorised, requires that the holder be of good repute, have 'adequate financial resources', have facilities for proper maintenance, and to ensure that drivers' hours regulations are not breached. It is also necessary to hold, or to employ as manager someone who holds a Certificate of Professional Competence (a basic qualification, obtained in the UK by a multiple-choice examination conducted by the Royal Society

---

[10] R.J. Balcombe, A.J. Astrop and R.D. Fairhead, *Bus competition in Great Britain since 1986: A national review*, Crowthorne, Berkshire: Transport Research Laboratory, 1992.

of Arts, or by exemption through holding other qualifications; it requires some cognizance of the regulations, of relevant law and of simple accountancy and business procedures). The licence is administered in the UK by quasi-judicial regional authorities (the Traffic Commissioners), which have survived from the 1930 licensing system, and which have a justified reputation for maintaining safety and professional standards. The Department of Transport supervises the condition of the vehicles, with draconian powers to deal with breaches of the regulations concerning construction and use. The Operator's Licence, loss of which would have a direct impact on the holder's business, is the means by which standards of quality are maintained.

Quality Licensing, Quantity Control, and a Contestable Market
Quality licensing is necessary in a 'fail-dangerous' industry, where technology prevents the maxim *caveat emptor* from protecting the interests of the consumer, let alone those of third parties and, for that matter, of employees. It must of course be a serious, if neglected, aspect of competition policy to ensure that quality control is not allowed to become unduly restrictive, or even obscurantist, so as to favour incumbents or to stifle technical initiative. There is no doubt that the dead hand of bureaucracy, whether from Whitehall or Brussels, remains open to criticism on this count, a recent example being an EC regulation which would restrict express coach speeds in such a way as to give protection to the railways.[11] But the former licensing system was chiefly criticised because of its provisions for quantity control, which virtually denied contestability for the line-haul sector[12] of the industry. (The price control that was removed in 1980 had been introduced without parliamentary power to deal with the monopolies created by the 1930 route licensing system.) That the industry now has no overt form of quantity control does not, however, mean that it approaches full contestability.

A key characteristic of a contestable market is the possibility of hit-and-run competition. The need for quality control

[11] Express coach services, other than for tourists, are virtually unknown in the EC outside the UK and Ireland.

[12] 'Line-haul' is a convenient short-hand term for the provision of regular services as distinct from 'charter' operation of individual trips. Both terms are current US usage.

limits access to firms that hold a valid Operator's Licence, and whose vehicles satisfy the regulations. Apart from the need to ensure that such regulations are not obscurantist, as some are, there are few objections to such a constraint.[13] Opponents of the 1985 Act argued that deregulation would flood the streets with 'pirates', who would destabilise the provision of services. While their arguments should never have been taken seriously, the present author was among those who recommended a registration system, at least for the initial period after greater contestability had been introduced, on the argument that sudden and rapid change could be expected to cause confusion, by lowering the already poor standards of marketing communication in the industry.[14] In the event, this reservation has been justified, at least in the short run.

The 1985 Act replaced the former quantity licence, which had defined the route and frequency of a service, and which had been granted only upon 'evidence of need',[15] with a system whereby it is necessary to register 'local services' which are up to 15 miles in length. (The express coach services thus do not have to be registered.) A registration cannot be refused by the Traffic Commissioner, unless steps have been taken to prohibit a recalcitrant firm from registering local services in a specified area, or at all. The registration has to specify the route, stopping places (including sections that are to be 'hail-and-ride'), timetable or frequency, and the maximum seating capacity of the vehicles to be used.

Thus limits on contestability arise from the bureaucratic hurdle and from the need to show one's hand to the competition. But there is also a requirement to give 42 days' notice when registering a new service, making substantial alterations to an existing registered service, or withdrawing it entirely. The ostensible purpose of the 42-day rule is to provide a signal to the authority responsible for subsidising 'socially necessary' services, which may decide to call for tenders to replace all or part of a service that is to be reduced or abandoned.

There are considerable differences between the practice of the authorities (county and regional councils and the

---

[13] The EC regulations concerning drivers' hours of work are notoriously problematic.

[14] See above, page 43.

[15] This was the 'road service licence', as described in the author's Hobart Paper No.23, *Transport for Passengers* (1963, revised edition 1971).

conurbation Passenger Transport Executives) responsible for providing this safety net of tendered services, should commercial considerations fail to satisfy a residual demand.

In rural areas, where profits have always been small, the remaining provision may indeed be largely dependent on subsidy, although this may still blanket potential innovation by private firms. Some councils, notably Gwynedd and Derbyshire, seem to seek to be bus operators by proxy, requiring successful franchisees to display the council's logo or even to paint part of the bus in the council's livery. (The franchisee must of course comply with the timetable laid down by the authority, and in cases where the authority receives all the revenue, must charge the fares provided for in the franchise.) Others, with minimal administrative cost, have a reactive policy of filling gaps, in contrast with those that seek responsibility for an entire network. Many, having no incentive to economise in the use of public funds, pay bus companies to carry air.

In urban areas, the provision of non-commercial services, however defined, presents different problems. We have already seen that some tenders call for fares lower than the market would support. To provide a subsidised service that doubles the frequency of a commercial one, and that undercuts its prices as well, is getting close to anti-competitive behaviour which tendering authorities are required by the Act to avoid. So also is the practice of subsidising a service over the whole of a route, where the original operator has decided for commercial reasons to cut it back at the outer end. The extent to which subsidy is necessary in urban areas is open to question, and some operators have sought to avoid leaving 'gaps' that might be filled by competitors by way of the tendering system.

Subsidy by Tender Regressive

In the absence of data, it seems likely that the system of subsidy by tender is to a greater or lesser extent regressive, as in the case of rail subsidy examined by Pryke and Dodgson.[16] Commercial bus operation has tended to concentrate on 'areas of low owner-occupation and low car-ownership',[17] so

[16] See above, page 31.

[17] Pickup *et al.*, *op. cit.*, p.153.

that much tendered operation benefits the better-off areas of towns. (The same may not be true of rural services.) The whole subject warrants investigation, if only to ensure that value is being obtained for the subsidy payments. A *prima facie* case exists for assuming that, were the tendering system to be withdrawn, commercial operators would fill any real gaps that might be left. There can be no justification for subsidising buses which carry few passengers.

A different effect of the subsidy provisions of the Act has been the opportunity for small firms to gain experience of line-haul operation, and then to register commercial services themselves. In this way the system has improved contestability, a notable example being a family business in rural Warwickshire which used the experience to challenge successfully the incumbent with high-frequency services on the streets of Birmingham, creating a competitive presence which they have been able to maintain.

The outcome of the 1980 and 1985 legislation, then, has been to make more contestable a market where management had been debilitated by 50 years of protection; to restore managerial autonomy and the discipline of the market; and, thus far, to give rise to an element of confusion where before there was imposed regularity and order. In addition, the primary objective of reducing subsidy has been substantially achieved, and cost efficiency has been greatly improved. Less than five years have passed since the new régime became fully effective, and that is a short enough time for spontaneous order to emerge in a market still distorted by wholly irrational capitalisation (an issue to which we shall return, below, pp.80-81). But enough has been said for the reader to assess what substance there may be in the pronouncement of the Labour Party's transport spokesman that 'all in all it's been pretty bloody disastrous'.[18]

The 1985 Act—Success or Failure?

Attempts to judge the success or failure of the 1985 legislation by national statistical measures become increasingly fruitless as the passage of time sees the introduction of new and exogenous developments. That the secular fall in the volume of bus travel, temporarily stemmed by massive subsidies

[18] Quoted in *Bus Business*, 15 December 1990.

between 1968 and 1986, has recommenced is plainly true, even though some firms have succeeded in bucking the trend. The latest figures[19] suggest a slight easing of the rate of decline, passenger journeys having fallen by less than 5 per cent in 1991, compared with an annual average fall of more than 10 per cent over the previous 10 years. (Journeys by coach increased by more than 4 per cent.) But so long as such figures are looked at in isolation from the general issue of mobility, any conclusions can only be partial.

The bus is the one form of transport which should be complementary to the private car or the taxi. Neither railways nor light rapid transit can ever cater for more than a minority of demand, and that at exorbitant expense. To the extent that they attract passengers from cars and buses, new car traffic will arrive to fill the road space thus made available—until it is priced in some way at the point of use. One objective of policy should therefore be to ensure that the bus is able to function in the most effective way to satisfy the demand for mobility. Experience has shown that this means a market dispensation for the industry.

Among those who deplore the Ridley reforms there are many who place bureaucratic tidiness above the merits of the market process, and others who see public transport as an instrument of social policy. There is evidence of value-judgements which place the car lower in esteem than the bus, and certainly lower than the train. There is thus a constituency ill-disposed to the creativity of the market and reluctant to accept that any benefit could flow from its restoration. It is interesting, though disturbing, to note the inclusion of some consumer representative organisations, such as 'Buswatch' and the National Federation of Bus Users, in this lobby. In the perfectly respectable activity of recording the weaknesses of the deregulated industry these pressure groups tend to forget those of the preceding era of protection, and too often fail to see the wood for the trees. There is a similar impression of *parti pris* judgement in the publications of the Association of Metropolitan Authorities,[20] which should not be accepted without reservation, applying as they do to a specific sector of the industry only.

[19] *Transport Statistics Great Britain 1992*, London: HMSO, 1992.

[20] See, for example, *Oiling the Wheels - A Transport Policy Statement*, Association of Metropolitan Authorities, 1987.

Criticism of the Ridley Reforms

The orchestrated and strident criticism of the liberalised régime conveys the impression that the critics would be better able to arrange the supply of bus services in accordance with passengers' demand (or 'need') than managers whose commercial survival requires it. But such lobbyists lay themselves open to accusations of rent-seeking,[21] for Mr Ridley's mine blew away many jobs among the local authorities that had, before 1986, been the proxy customers of the industry.

Not every comment on the Ridley reforms has been overtly critical. John Kay and David Thompson, in a recent paper, remark that 'the evidence suggests that there has been a significant change in incumbents' performance, even where entry has not altered market structure'.[22] But as the 1985 Act passed through Parliament it was subjected to strident and emotional attack by people who had a vested interest in the former dispensation. Fortunately the chaos they predicted did not materialise, which is itself a mark of the success of the new régime. Mileage cuts were far less than had been expected, and total vehicle mileage rose, as shown in Table 6, although passenger usage fell. Buses continued to run to published timetables (even if these were just as difficult to obtain) instead of becoming 'irregular and sporadic'. While their average age increased, the safety and comfort of buses was maintained through the enforcement of the quality regulations. One glorious piece of nonsense appeared in the publicity of a county council, where it was forecast that there would be an increased burden on the ratepayer, because of the need to 'subsidise uneconomic services without the benefit of income from profitable routes', while going on to say that 60 per cent of the existing network was 'uneconomic'. Where the supposed cross-subsidy had been coming from it did not say.[23]

But it is not enough to show that the atavistic fears played

[21] See below, note 13, page 84.

[22] J. Kay and D. Thompson, 'Regulatory Reform in the United Kingdom: Principles and Application', in D. Banister & K. Button (eds.), *Transport in a Free Market Economy*, London: Macmillan, 1991, p.27. The term 'Regulatory Reform', to include both deregulation and privatisation, is a useful contribution.

[23] This hoary old chestnut had been disposed of long since: see G.J. Ponsonby, 'What is an Unremunerative Service?', *Institute of Transport Journal*, 1963.

upon by politically motivated and rent-seeking opposition were unfounded. That was already plain to the disinterested observer in 1984. The positive consequences of the legislation may not lend themselves to generalisation, but they are real enough.

One immediate effect of the legislation was a return to plant bargaining, which undoubtedly kept many jobs in existence which had been under threat. The former National Agreements had tended to make wages too high in the North and too low in the South, but their most significant effects followed from their extensive clauses governing hours and conditions of service (outwith the statutory drivers' hours regulations), which left little room for flexibility of employment. At 'D-Day' the employers' representatives walked out of the National Councils, and the system collapsed.

The acceptance in Britain of the minibus as a form of urban transport (long found in cities as European as Buenos Aires) has been attributed to deregulation. But the original experiment in Exeter was backed by the National Bus Company, and began before the 1985 Act was passed. What is true is that deregulation made it much easier for small buses on high-frequency services to be introduced—a style of operation which often leads to startling increases in traffic. Sadly, not every manager seems to have grasped the principles of minibus operation, which require a substantial departure from traditional practices—such high frequencies obviate the necessity of a timetable, for example, and no fixed stops are required in residential areas for 'hail and ride' services.[24] The further potential of minibuses is considerable; their introduction in Portsmouth is reported to have increased bus use by 60 per cent.[25]

Consequences for Management

One consequence of regulatory reform was a thorough-going shake-out of middle management. A measure of the previous bureaucratisation of the industry is that it has been able to perform so well with a greatly reduced administrative 'tail'; as Table 7 shows, the average number of employees per bus fell by some 25 per cent between 1978 and 1990/91 (from 2·9 to

[24] See P. Fawcett, *Minibuses*, Kingston upon Thames, Surrey: Croner, 1989.

[25] Verbatim report in *Transport Week*, 20 July 1991.

2·2). Another was the early retirement of senior managers who did not feel they could come to terms with the market (a not unreasonable decision for those who adhered sincerely to the paternalistic ethos of the post-war years). For those who remained, a fairly drastic paradigm shift was required, as explained in a recent study.[26]

TABLE 7
EMPLOYEES PER BUS: GREAT BRITAIN, 1978-1991

Year	Vehicles (000s)	Employees (000s)	Employees per vehicle
1978	73·8	211·1	2·9
1979	72·9	208·9	2·9
1980	69·1	201·5	2·9
1981	69·9	190·9	2·7
1982	70·7	187·7	2·7
1983	70·2	187·4	2·7
1984	68·8	181·5	2·6
1985/86	67·9	174·2	2·6
1986/87	69·6	166·7	2·4
1987/88	71·7	159·8	2·2
1988/89	72·2	159·6	2·2
1989/90	72·9	158·6	2·2
1990/91	78·1	155·5	2·2

Source: *Transport Statistics Great Britain 1992*, London: HMSO, 1992, Tables 5.4 and 5.8.

The general conclusion of the study was that benefits have started to flow, but that there is still room for improvement as the remaining effects of the product-driven ethos of the previous era continue to die away. With some exceptions, managers no longer see transport as a social service, though a few may think that it should be. From the sample it appears

[26] Reported in J. Hibbs, 'An Evaluation of Urban Bus Deregulation in Britain: A Survey of Management Attitudes', *Progress in Planning*, Vol.36, Part 3, 1991.

[60]

that job-satisfaction has substantially increased, because of the removal of subsidy and thus the power it had consequently given to local authorities. It is now implicitly assumed that bus operation has become an industry, in that insights and terminology proper to commercial management are taken for granted.

Changes reported were greatest in the area of human resource management, vehicle policy and service design and delivery. Publicity and advertising were admitted to have declined from a previously poor standard. The weakest area was identified as a general lack of understanding of marketing management, combined with an unreadiness to develop discriminatory pricing beyond a crude 'peak/off peak' distinction. This was coupled with a reliance on the system-wide travelcard, which was seen as a means to attain market dominance, as well as a source of valuable up-front revenue.[27] If managers of bus companies continue to become market-led rather than product-driven as in the past, consumers will have much for which to thank the Ridley reforms. A very high proportion of those interviewed in the study said they would prefer to continue in the market economy rather than move to any form of franchise.

The Need for Further Action

There must be serious reservations whether regulatory reform went far enough to permit the maximum liberty for a functioning market. Thus there are a number of steps that remain to be taken if mobility is to be available in response to demand, and not as felt suitable by bureaucrats or politicians. Before these are considered, a word must be said about weaknesses in marketing, identified in the study of management responses to regulatory reform.[28]

Despite notable exceptions, the product-driven approach of the regulated age has yet to give way wholeheartedly to the market-led attitudes appropriate to management in the new era. There have been complaints that managers have abused their new-found freedom by indulging in over-frequent

---

[27] Dr Glaister remarks of the London Travelcard that 'For all its advantages, it does confound the price system because the holder faces no charge for the additional trips he makes'. (S. Glaister, in *Transport Options for London*, London School of Economics, 1991, p.96.)

[28] See above, note 26, p.60.

change. Such complaints appear to be justified in many places. Though buses should not run on 'invisible tramlines', as they did for so long, in any market consumers need to know what is on offer, so some degree of stability is desirable. Apart from getting this balance right, through the development of marketing research and market intelligence, good publicity and promotion are required, though neither is widely to be found.

Moreover, in a competitive market producers will often discriminate in both price and quality, by market segment; yet such developments have been very slow to appear. Evidence is scarce, but little is heard of the costing skills which must underpin marketing management of this kind. If there is one sinister hangover from the industry's 50 years of price regulation it is the practice of standard charging (the same rate per mile over a whole system), and the crude assumption that mileage earning less than average revenue for the firm is making a loss, that for so long went with it.[29] It is against these concerns that the initiative of the Bus & Coach Council to develop marketing strategies for the industry is to be welcomed.

Problems with Travelcards and Tendered Services

Linked inevitably with pricing policy is the widespread use of the Travelcard.[30] By making the marginal cost of each trip zero, the cards inhibit price discrimination, except where 'off-peak' cards provide for it in a crude form. Since the price of the card reflects an average length of trip, they must also undercharge for longer distances, and overcharge for shorter ones (where cash payment becomes an alternative). However, the development of the all-purpose 'decremental chip card', already on the horizon, offers the possibility of returning to a creative pricing strategy: the trade press is already examining its implications.[31]

---

[29] Professor Gwilliam disposed of this argument some time ago: see K.M. Gwilliam, *Transport and Public Policy*, London: Allen & Unwin, 1964, p.32.

[30] See above, note 27, p.61.

[31] See *Automatic Ticketing and Revenue Collecting*, Autumn/Winter 1991/92. These stored value cards (or 'electronic purses') are already familiar in the form of the phone card, and they are expected to include payment before long for such things as parking meters, taxi fares and even admission to cinemas - as well as train and bus trips. The first use of the system is being explored by the Greater Manchester Passenger Transport Executive.

There are also problems deriving from the legislation itself and from the policies of the Office of Fair Trading (OFT). Services provided by tender to local authorities have come to form a distinct element in the market, whose design and delivery cannot be judged against any objective criteria.

That is not surprising, because the arguments for providing 'socially necessary services' turn eventually upon the concept of 'social justice', which Hayek has argued convincingly to be an empty formula, 'intellectually disreputable' and incompatible with the preservation of a peaceful society of free men and women.[32] An understandable concern lest the Act should cause substantial numbers to suffer a sharp reduction in mobility has endowed the authorities concerned with power to intervene in the market process, despite the saving clause in the Act which requires them

'so to conduct themselves as not to inhibit competition between persons providing or seeking to provide public passenger transport services in their area'.[33]

Two points are at issue, one of principle and both of practical significance. The first is the logical weakness of the clause, which is concerned with the subsidiary matter of competition at the expense of the re-instatement of the market (the real objective of the Act). The second is the way in which the loophole thus created has enabled decisions to be taken that undermine the market process itself.

For the system of subsidy by tender has been used by many if not most authorities to continue the use of the bus as a form of social service. Since there is not (and cannot be) any rigorous measure of the value of social services, the provision of subsidised bus services depends effectively on the available financial resources, allocated by an evaluation of 'need' reached by the administrators of the system, with the elected representatives behind them. The effect of competitive tendering is likely to be to keep costs down. But it is plain that, especially in periods of stringency, available funds (constrained by 'rate-capping') will always be fully spent.

[32] See 'The Atavism of Social Justice', Hayek's R.C. Mills Memorial Lecture, reprinted in F.A. Hayek, *New Studies in Philosophy, Politics, Economics and the History of Ideas*, London: Routledge & Kegan Paul, 1978.

[33] Transport Act 1985, Section 93(1).

Market Supply Stifled by Tendering?

A side-effect of the tendering process is the inhibition of supply which would otherwise appear spontaneously through the market process. Section 92(1) of the Act applies only to persons providing or actively *seeking* to provide bus services—not to a situation in which an entrepreneur is considering whether or not to seek to do so. There is historical evidence that in a competitive market firms may seek out under-provided routes, neglected by the larger operators with higher costs.[34] Such a process will not necessarily produce services to coincide with those considered suitable by the bureaucratic administrators.

Still more serious is the way the tendering system works when its administrators see fit to fill gaps which they perceive in commercial provision. Some firms have perhaps been over-cautious in deciding to abandon evening and Sunday services which others in similar circumstances have successfully maintained. Where the local authority has called for tenders to replace such services, different firms are likely to take over more or less of the mileage concerned. As a result, there may be as many as three firms operating on the same route at different times, which passengers find confusing. It does not even follow that a combined timetable will be available, and because of rulings by the OFT no such firm may accept return tickets issued by another. (The paradox of OFT intervention to impede the market process is examined below, pp.65-67.)

The '42-day rule', on the other hand, does not seem to have had an enervating effect on the market process. Indeed, it does not seem to have had much effect at all, apart from causing a great deal of unnecessary paperwork. Its abolition would make the market marginally more contestable, and if the tendering process must continue, the indication of impending change could be achieved by requiring notice to be given in the local press; the registration of local bus services would in that case have to continue, unnecessary though it is; if the tendering system is itself unnecessary, then no problem remains.

To the extent that market failures exist in the wake of the Ridley reforms, they often reflect the residual regulations,

---

[34] See the present author's article, 'The London Independent Bus Operators 1922-1934', in *Transport History*, Vol.5, 1972.

or the necessarily disturbing outcomes of dismantling the system of protectionism in force for the previous 55 years. But the situation has not been improved by the policies of the Office of Fair Trading, which was required to 'hit the ground running' when the bus industry lost its exemption from the Restrictive Practices Act 1976 under Clause 115 of the Transport Act 1985.

The tendency of many larger bus companies to seek territorial monopoly has to be faced by any regulator, not least because such behaviour was positively encouraged under the former regulatory system and because it is favoured by those who attach value to 'the network'.

When authorising the sale of the subsidiaries of the National Bus Company and the Scottish Bus Group, the Secretaries of State followed a policy designed to produce a 'patchwork quilt', so that the emerging ownership groups should not be allowed to acquire too many neighbouring companies. But this could only provide for the original pattern; any tendency to depart from it by sale and purchase is the concern of the OFT which has to decide what would amount to a dominant position in any part of the market. From the start the OFT has found such decisions very difficult. In the case of one firm in the Midlands, where an acquisition was called in question, it made itself look foolish; other cases have gone to appeal; and even where divestment has been required, the industry has not even today identified any broadly acceptable basis for the OFT's decisions. A recent announcement that is taken to bar bus operators from acquiring rail franchises (in their own territory) under the Government's privatisation proposals underlines the need for OFT policies to be reviewed.

The 'Public Interest' and the OFT

The ultimate cause of the problem is the requirement that the OFT must look to 'the public interest', a concept that any economist should distrust—for how can it be measured?—and which had proved the central weakness of the former system of road service licensing, permitting wide inconsistencies in decision-making. There is no space here for an extended analysis of activities of bus firms that the Director-General regards as suspect, but the more serious are perhaps those related to pricing (an area where, as we have seen, managers have so far themselves been unready to innovate). 'Agreements not to encroach', which the OFT sees as 'significantly anti-competitive',[35] can and no doubt do exist, as the result of unrecorded negotiations in remote hostelries; Adam Smith's remarks about the anti-competitive aspects of the social activities of businessmen certainly apply to bus managers today, and the OFT can neither police nor prevent them.

Pricing is a different matter, for the OFT gives the game away in the publication noted above. It states:

'Agreements between bus operators to charge particular fares or to establish common fare zones or structures are generally anti-competitive (*except in the sort of arrangement involving travelcard schemes*)'.[36]

This exception opens the door to the use of travelcards themselves as anti-competitive weapons, though not always with complete success.[37]

The OFT here demonstrates some confusion of thought but a more serious criticism of the travelcard, which it also neglects, is its effect in blanketing any form of discriminatory pricing. It is a form of standard charging, the practice that did so much to undermine the finances of the bus industry during the era of price control between 1930 and 1980.[38] The extra attraction of substantial advance revenue means that the bus industry must look askance at any criticism of the travelcard, but it remains an extraordinary inconsistency of OFT policy thus to give it its positive blessing.

It is to be expected that bus companies will exploit any opportunity to regain the perceived advantages of monopoly. There are two examples which require further legislative attention. One is the very recent practice of bringing a passing-

[35] OFT, *Restrictive Trade Practices in the Bus Industry*, London: HMSO, 1991.

[36] *Ibid.*, p.6 (my italics).

[37] A travelcard available for the services of one firm, or a group of firms, is an investment on the part of the passenger, who will be discouraged from paying again to ride on a competitor's bus. It is, however, possible for a competitor to make a living from fares for trips too short to justify the investment.

[38] I have been able to find no authority in the legislation for the practice of endorsing a fare table as a condition of the road service licence, which was the Traffic Commissioners' practice until 1980.

off action[39] where a competitor uses the plaintiff's route number or numbers, with or without a distinguishing letter suffix. Because it is not necessary to prove fraudulent motive or misrepresentation, such cases are almost impossible to defend, yet their outcome is clearly an absurdity, preventing passengers from discovering conveniently where a bus might take them.

Predatory Activities in the Bus Industry

More drastic, but no less significant for the free working of the market, is the potential for the larger firms to engage in predatory activities, of which the most serious is the use of their greater financial resources to drive a newcomer out of business (or 'to make him an offer that he cannot afford to refuse' to sell up). Predation may involve practices that go back to horse-bus days—'racing and chasing', 'hanging back', and so forth. In so far as these are dangerous, the parties concerned can be effectively disciplined in the terms of the Operator's Licence which they must hold, for which they are responsible to the Regional Traffic Commissioner. But prices are uncontrolled, and serious undercutting can usually be sustained longer by the large firm than the small (although the small firm may have some advantage by way of lower overhead costs).

Other things being equal, it would be for the market to determine whether the small or the large firm is the more efficient. There is reason to believe that competition on a given route can increase overall demand, perhaps because frequency is a quality of service that is valued in the market. This would lead to the conclusion that the cost of driving out a competitor by severe under-pricing will not be recouped by returning to the *status quo ante*. But while theory indicates that predatory pricing is ineffective, it is by no means plain that all bus managers have understood it, for their actions indicate rather an atavistic desire to protect their territory at all costs.

The fear of predatory pricing does not seem to have inhibited small firms from entering the market, with varying success (and sometimes with vehicles that deserve the adjective

[39] 'An action brought against a person for having represented the marks on, set-up, packaging or other features of his goods, as being those of the plaintiff, and having caused the plaintiff actual or probable loss thereby.' (*Oxford Companion to Law*, Oxford, 1980, p.933.)

'decrepit'). As we have seen,[40] 'a dynamic state of equilibrium' seems to exist, and while powers to penalise the anti-competitive use of pricing could no doubt be put in place, providing for exemplary damages against the predator,[41] it is to be hoped that the understanding of market processes will lead to further enlightenment among managers as to their self-interest in this field.

Yet when all the necessary reforms have been completed, and the market for bus and coach operations has been made as contestable as such a programme permits, there remains one further problem: the severe congestion that besets the highway, resulting from the Englishman's supposed right to 'the freedom of the road'. Upon the solution to this problem any policy for mobility must turn.

---

[40] See above, p.52.

[41] A sudden reduction of fares below a bench-mark proportion of those applying generally in the predator's operations would be *prima facie* evidence, while their subsequent increase after the withdrawal of the plaintiff's service would present an 'open-and-shut case'.

IV. ROAD-USE PRICING

An Idea Whose Time Has Come

Early in the study of economics, students learn that one of the functions of prices is to reconcile supply and demand. Rising prices, due to scarcity of a commodity, attract additional supply, and first satisfy and then reduce demand. There are few examples of scarcity in the past 50 years that have not been followed within a decade by a glut. However, one area where the process can function erratically is in the supply of land—Mark Twain summed it up when he said:

> 'If they ask me what to put their money in, I tell 'em, land. I have it on the best authority they ain't makin' any more.'

The limited supply of land is also affected by social pressures. Political opposition to the construction of motorways repeats the experience of 19th-century railway promoters, so that the two systems took much the same length of time to complete.[1] The NIMBY factor (Not In My Back Yard) was not unknown in the 1840s. But it is the supply of land for urban uses that causes the most serious problems today.

One of the historic benefits of city life is the proximity of social and commercial satisfactions. This gives rise to a centripetal force that leads to constant pressure on the supply of land. For thousands of years the boundary of the city was set by walking distances, and it was not until urban passenger transport appeared (the omnibus was introduced in London in 1829) that the growth of cities could be accommodated by their spatial extension. Rail commuting, which came later, was followed by the tramway, electrified around the end of the century, and the motor bus followed, developing rapidly after 1919. The car is thus an extension of a centrifugal force which has offset the older trend for cities to be compact, with a dense occupation of land.

[1] Taking 1835 as the start of the Railway Age, almost all English towns of any size were connected by rail by 1855 (M. Robbins, *The Railway Age*, London: Routledge & Kegan Paul, 1962). The comparable period for completion of the basic motorway system is 1958 to 1980.

Left alone, it seems that the centrifugal force has the greater power. Los Angeles has become a car city, with its land used as to one-third each for highways, buildings and parking lots. The Angeleños accepted this with little opposition, and it only became a political issue when growing congestion reached the stage of 'gridlock', with cars no longer able to move on the 'freeways'. In most cities, the market for land has been constrained by zoning or some other form of social control, yet everywhere congestion has become a growing problem.

A market that is constrained can still function: the price of urban land continues to reflect the values placed upon it in various uses. There may be a case for intervention to provide public open space, where the opportunity cost of such use cannot be covered by entry charges. But land for transport uses is a special case, raising issues that, while fundamental, have attracted little concern. The special characteristic of land required for the movement of people and goods in British towns and cities is that its capital earns no income, and appears on no balance sheet; it is as if the value of such land did not exist.

By a Treasury convention, land in the ownership of a nationalised business trading at a loss does not appear in its accounts. And the 'ownership' of land for road transport—the ownership of the roads—is highly debatable.[2] Only land acquired under statute for the construction of Trunk Roads or Special Roads (motorways) can be said to be in the beneficial ownership of even a public authority. Other roads appear to be no more than 'rights of passage' over land that belongs to the frontagers (as to which they have no rights and but limited duties). Thus, just as with railways, the capital value of roads appears in no-one's set of accounts.

Congestion and the Market

Since roads do not really belong to anyone, it is not surprising that they are used wastefully. This conclusion led the present author to specify road-use pricing as an *a priori* requirement for the successful return of the bus industry to the market, by regulatory reform and privatisation.[3] Plainly, there must be serious imperfections in the market for mobility so long as there

---

[2] See J. Hibbs and G. Roth, *Tomorrow's Way: Managing Roads in a Free Society*, London: Adam Smith Institute, 1992.

[3] See John Hibbs, *Transport Without Politics...?*, Hobart Paper 95, *op. cit.*

is no market for the use of road space, which at certain times and places is an exceedingly scarce commodity. One consequence is the weakness of the bus as an alternative to other modes of passenger transport.

Street congestion is no new phenomenon; it was prevalent in ancient Rome, and not unknown in 17th-century London. In the early years of the 20th century it was described in terms that would be appropriate today.[4] Photographs from the 1920s show the streets of central London packed solid—with buses.

Today the problem arises from people's choice of the car for access to their satisfactions, and the growth of a 'consumer economy' which requires high standards of distribution, and the consequent expansion of commercial transport. The effect on the bus has been disastrous, not least because of a 'ratchet effect'[5] which prevents operators from exploiting fully the spatial economy that the bus can offer. A situation of equal misery then tends to arise.

Zero Marginal Price for Highway Use

This apparently 'no-win' situation is in fact easily analysed in economic terms: with the exception of the occasional toll for a river crossing, the unit price of using the highway is *zero at the margin*. In this situation, which is also common for domestic water supply, the user has no incentive to economise, and, price being zero, demand expands and always appears to be in excess of supply. Thus the solution, as Professor Reuben Smeed's committee concluded nearly 30 years ago,[6] is to introduce some form of pricing, at times and places in which severe congestion arises.

The force of Smeed's argument has grown with time, and the development of electronic devices has made his proposed solution both cheaper and more effective.[7] Smeed concluded

---

[4] *Report of the Royal Commission appointed to inquire into and report upon the means of Locomotion and Transport in London*, Vol. I, Cd. 2597, London: HMSO, 1905.

[5] The marginal passenger who first transfers from bus to car experiences a significant net gain in utility, which is then reduced for each successive passenger until congestion has an equalising effect. The ratchet comes into effect since there is no corresponding gain for the marginal car user who transfers back to the bus.

[6] *Road Pricing: The Economic and Technical Possibilities* (the Smeed Report), London: HMSO, 1964.

[7] For a recent extensive treatment of the subject, see D. Bayliss *et al.*, *Paying for Progress*, London: Chartered Institute of Transport, 1990; and a supplementary report of 1992.

that fuel taxation is a crude form of rationing (it would certainly not overcome the ratchet effect). He also rejected any form of tolled cordon as failing to pick up those whose homes are inside it. Instead, he envisaged a solid-state device placed in the vehicle, into which would slot a prepaid 'smart card', whose value would be diminished ('decremented') each time the vehicle passed over or near to an induction coil (set in the road, like those which activate traffic lights), or a beacon placed at the roadside. The coils or beacons would be activated by growing congestion, and would be neutral at other times. A sealed lamp in the box, visible outside the vehicle, would be illuminated to indicate an offence if there were no valid card in place, enabling enforcement on the same lines as that for an expired tax disk.

A variety of systems for selective road user charging has emerged since the publication of the Smeed Report. In 1975 the Singapore government introduced an area licensing system which reduced the peak flow of cars into the city centre by almost 40 per cent. Such methods of rationing capacity, which may be suitable where the problem is access to the central business district, are unlikely to help where congestion exists over a wider area. Between 1983 and 1985 an electronic road pricing system was operated in Hong Kong, although no charge was made; such systems have thus been shown to be technically feasible. The Hong Kong system, however, had two serious drawbacks, which must be avoided if road-use pricing is to be economically effective and socially acceptable.

The first is that payment must be at the point of use. A monthly or quarterly account will have no rationing effect worth speaking of, as is well illustrated by the way we pay for our telephone calls. A decremental card, slotted into a box which emits an audible tone when passing an activated coil or beacon, will bring home to the user that money has been spent. A further argument for the smart card is that the alternative implies an electronically identifiable number plate, recognition of which feeds information into the computer that finally produces the account. It is unlikely that public opinion would be happy with the idea that one's journeys could be identified in this way.

Road Pricing to Allocate Scarce Space

Much opposition to road pricing assumes that it is a tax on

mobility, whereas it is of course a means of allocating a scarce commodity. Variable prices for foodstuffs do not amount to a tax, even though prices rise and fall according to quantities coming into the market. Schemes such as those introduced in Bergen and Oslo have the disadvantage in economic terms of being a form of taxation, and not a method of bringing costs home, through pricing, to the vehicle user.[8] A scheme proposed for Cambridge suffers from the same weakness, as well as taking the form of a perimeter cordon. It is perhaps true that any form of road-use pricing is a least-worst solution to the congestion problem, at least until an equity can be introduced into the road system, so that prices can reflect capital values.

The feasibility of electronic point-of-use road pricing is now beyond doubt. Its political acceptability is growing, as congestion becomes an ever greater issue. The Government's endorsement of it is shown by the expected publication of a Green Paper. It has a further attraction in terms of environmental pollution, for its purpose is to reduce the amount of time that vehicles spend stationary in traffic. It is no more inequitable than the pricing system for food, and by enabling the bus to function more efficiently it makes a positive contribution to the welfare of those who do not use cars. If its introduction were to be accompanied by reduction of the excise duty (the so-called 'Road Fund Licence') to the administration costs of the licence disk, the system would be seen as 'fair'. There would be the further benefit of reducing the relative cost of motoring for people in rural areas, where public transport is never likely to be satisfactory. Ideally, the authority managing the system should be outwith the public sector borrowing requirement (PSBR), and able to borrow forward on its substantial future cash flow, so as to invest in improvements to the infrastructure that would benefit those who chose not to pay the road-use price.

It will be recognised that such a policy implies something close to the notion of 'earmarked taxes', or hypothecated revenue, which the Treasury regards with disapproval.[9] But it

[8] See D. Bayliss *et al.*, Supplement to *Paying for Progress*, London: Chartered Institute of Transport, 1992. These systems were designed to generate funds for major road investment, without significantly affecting the volume of traffic entering the city centre.

[9] Ranjit S. Teja, and Barry Bracewell-Milnes, *The Case for Earmarked Taxes: Government Spending and Public Choice*, Research Monograph 46, London: Institute of Economic Affairs, 1991.

cannot be too strongly emphasised that the idea is to price the use of scarce road space, not to tax it. (The message may not yet have got through to the motorists' organisations.) And it is surely reasonable that the revenue arising from such pricing should be at the disposal of the organisation which sets the level of charge.

Our present method of using inherently scarce road space gives rise to inefficiencies arising from congestion and the 'ratchet effect'.[10] When uninformed choice is replaced by an effective pricing mechanism there will be a period of adjustment, as people react to the new régime. For some there will be gains, and for others losses, but in the outcome there must be a net benefit, as the various means to mobility are brought into balance, and the existing distortions in the market progressively disappear. Any constraint upon car use will give rise to claims that freedom of choice is being restricted. But it is the bus industry that has suffered most severely from the growth of street congestion, thereby weakening its ability to offer an acceptable alternative.

The Benefits of the Market

Any pricing system designed to reflect road scarcity will require heuristic calibration. That is to say, the rates charged will be arrived at by trial and error, until the result is a reasonably free flow of traffic on the previously congested sections of road. By then, indifferent demand will have shifted to alternative modes, different times, different routes, or, indeed, different destinations. Road users remaining will be those who value road space sufficiently to pay for it at the going rate. In the absence of an equity in the roads themselves,[11] the rate would not be completely determined by market forces, but it would serve as a proxy for them in tending to a more efficient use of the factor land. A *sine qua non* must be the removal of the charging authority from the control of the Treasury, which would otherwise undermine the whole advantage through its dislike of hypothecated revenue. It should also be open to private investors to enter the market, taking advantage of the pricing system to construct

[10] See above, note 5, p.71.

[11] This could be achieved by vesting the ownership of the roads in some kind of public body, with the option of subsequent privatisation: see J. Hibbs and G. Roth, *op. cit.*

by-passes and other improvements where the prospective revenues were attractive—a freedom which could well extend to the construction of busways.[12]

Buses and Coaches As 'Major Players'

The outcome of road pricing would undoubtedly be the restoration of bus and coach businesses as major players in the market for mobility. Provided the total package of reforms were regarded as equitable, there is reason to believe the majority of car users would not share the opposition of the motoring organisations: a survey in 1989 found only 24 per cent who said they would never use alternative transport to the private car.[13] As to the charge that road pricing would be socially divisive, a recent report concludes that

> '...as a rule of thumb...it seems that the direct effects of road user charges are likely to benefit the upper and lower ends of the income distribution curve with, all other things being equal, disbenefits most likely to those car users in the middle of the range who are most likely to have to change some of their travel arrangements.'[14]

This conclusion should be seen in the light of the growing number of car owners at the lower end of the curve (see Table 2, above, p.22).

More Free-Flowing Traffic

One result of road pricing would be a reasonably free flow of traffic at all times of the day. Roads would be busier at peak times than off-peak, but vehicles would not be held stationary or in slow-moving queues. Lapsed time for their journeys would be markedly reduced, and the ratchet effect[15] would be defeated. In that situation, the bus companies would benefit in two ways, provided they were ready to make the necessary investment— and to develop the necessary marketing skills.

In the first place, the running time required to cover a

[12] See above, p.35 and Box 1, pp.36-37.

[13] Department of the Environment, *Digest of Environmental Protection and Water Statistics*, London: HMSO, 1990.

[14] D. Bayliss *et al.*, Supplement to *Paying for Progress, op. cit.*, p.11.

[15] See above, note 5, p.71.

given distance would be substantially reduced. As a consequence, the number of buses and drivers needed for today's output would be fewer, offering savings on both capital and revenue account. (Practising managers have indicated that they might expect savings of the order of 25 per cent in conversation with the present author.) From such advantages the industry would be well placed to exploit its new position in the market.

Given a readiness to invest, bus companies would need to respond to the second consequence of road pricing by targetting production and fares much more closely to market segments than most of them have done in the past.[16] For the success of road pricing and the future prosperity of the bus industry alike depend upon the availability of an acceptable alternative to the private car as a means to mobility. The industry's trade association, the Bus & Coach Council, has already started to look to such an alternative with its 'Buses Mean Business' campaign, which has attracted funding from the Department of Transport for bus priority schemes and other kinds of improvement to the infrastructure. The competence of management in the industry is impressive; what road pricing requires is the ability to make an imaginative leap in order to benefit from the enormous opportunities that it would open. Then we could hope to see the bus, no longer a mass-producer of seat-miles, taking its place (in different forms for different market segments) as the principal complement and alternative to the car, as that in turn became 'just another means of transport'.

Road pricing would open the way to innovation, and the period since 1986 has shown that, in a market, many bus managers are good at innovating. The market must be kept contestable, keeping it open to new investment as new opportunities arise. Above all, road pricing must be introduced as a means of removing market imperfections, and not as a tax. In a recent article on the National Health Service[17] the author justly observes that '...a market is not about deterrence. It is about price-conscious choice. Paying may be painful but it brings with it the power to choose'. The argument for point-of-use electronic road-use pricing could hardly have been better put.

[16] See John Hibbs, *Marketing Management in the Bus and Coach Industry, op. cit.*, pp.39-47.

[17] David Green, 'The NHS Reforms: From ration-book collectivism to market socialism', *Economic Affairs*, Vol.12, No.3, 1992, pp.12-17, quotation cited from p.16.

V. THE NEXT STEPS

A Restatement of Principle

In a letter published in *The Independent* on 24 September 1991, the Director General of the Institution of Civil Engineers called for 'coherence and co-ordination' in transport policy, supporting a previous call from the Director General of the Confederation of British Industry. He wrote:

> 'At the national level a transport co-ordination group dealing with all modes of transport should be established, which would report directly to the Secretary of State within the framework of the Department of Transport. At regional level there should be regional transport committees reporting to the national committee, chaired by regional directors of the DoT and charged with the co-ordination of all modes of transport.'

Interestingly, he did not specifically include the private car among the modes to be co-ordinated.

Such a neo-socialist policy recommendation comes at a strange time, when the disasters of centralised transport planning in Eastern Europe have been opened to our view. As far as the bus industry is concerned, the Civil Engineers' proposals are close to those favoured by the Labour and Liberal Democrat parties, which would have regional authorities determining what buses should run, where and when, and at what fares. In the Labour scheme, acceptable firms (which would exclude small businesses) would be invited to tender at intervals for packages of routes, some likely to earn more than others, and during the period of their franchise there would be no possibility of competition. Whether any successful tenderer could survive the loss of such a franchise at the end of its term is doubtful (as the recent re-tendering of ITV franchises has shown), for what would it do with its vehicles and staff? Ironically, such franchisees would have to be subjected to regulation of the kind devised for the 'utilities'—gas, electricity, telephones and water—since they would enjoy an artificially created monopoly. What is being proposed is competition for a temporary monopoly, which is mercantilism in a thin disguise. Perhaps it is time for civil engineers and businessmen, not to mention politicians, to refresh their knowledge of economics.

The title of Gilbert Ponsonby's Hobart Paper, *Co-ordination through Competition*,[1] is a happy phrase for the sort of spontaneous order that we may confidently expect to emerge from the market process, in transport as in any market that is reasonably contestable. As Hayek remarks:[2]

> 'To the naive mind that can conceive of order only as the product of deliberate arrangement, it may seem absurd that in complex conditions order, and adaptation to the unknown, can be achieved more effectively by decentralising decisions, and that a division of authority will actually extend the possibility of overall order.'

The argument for a market for bus and coach transport could hardly be more cogently put. If any doubts remain in the reader's mind, then it should be sufficient to recall Hayek's further remark,[3] that

> '...dispersed knowledge is *essentially* dispersed, and cannot possibly be gathered together and conveyed to an authority charged with the task of deliberately creating order'.

Mr Ridley's Mine Frees the Market

The explosion of Mr Ridley's mine has had the entirely beneficial effect (outwith London) of freeing the market to do its work of 'co-ordinating' the manifold wants of all the players in it. It is beyond human capacity to create an extended order of this kind, and any attempt to control it introduces a clog on the free working of the process. While accepting that the 'fail-dangerous' nature of transport technology demands quality regulation,[4] the steps now required are to dismantle still further the barriers to contestability, not to regress to a situation in which bureaucrats in Bristol determine the bus service to be provided in West Cornwall (or even on the streets of Bristol itself).

---

[1] Hobart Paper No.49, *op. cit.*

[2] F.A. Hayek, *The Fatal Conceit*, London: Routledge, 1988, pp.76-77.

[3] *Loc. cit.* (emphasis in the original).

[4] See above, page 53.

A central planning authority could not identify the public transport requirements that would follow from the introduction of road pricing, for there can be no foreknowledge of the changes in travel patterns that would follow from it. In the market, entrepreneurs have a direct incentive to forecast the local situation, with financial penalties for getting their forecast wrong. Bureaucrats cannot take the risk involved in such a process, and in the absence of prospective rewards they have little incentive to get the forecast right.

This analysis of the situation is at odds with the views of the Association of Metropolitan Authorities, which have themselves been influential in public debate. It would be unfortunate if a consensus should prevail which results in loss of the opportunity that now exists to unify passenger transport policy around a market for road space. But the pronouncements of the Confederation of British Industry and the Institution of Civil Engineers[5] are not untypical of a school of thought that is profoundly opposed to a market solution to the transport problem. Those holding to the supposed virtues of planning should perhaps reflect upon the physicists' conclusion, that

> 'The only statements which can be made for chaotic systems are probabilistic ones, based on the inherent uncertainties in the initial conditions'.[6]

Civil Engineers' Blueprint Omits Motor Cars

As explained above, the Institution of Civil Engineers did not include the private car in their blueprint for co-ordination. But the demand for passenger transport is not bounded by any one mode; the *generic* demand is for mobility. In its purest form it might be defined as a wish to be able to maximise our marginal utility *somewhere else*, so that the ideal form of transport would be a vehicle into which we get (here) and get out (there) now; something we might call 'instantaneous

[5] See above, page 77.

[6] Peter Coveney and Roger Highfield, *The Arrow of Time*, Flamingo paperback, London: HarperCollins, 1991, p.346. This comment may be set beside Mr John Telford Beasley's rhetorical question *'Why plan at all?'* (the title of his keynote address to a Symposium at the University of Newcastle upon Tyne in 1990, reprinted in *London Lines*, Summer 1990).

transposition'. For the accepted definition of the product of transport is 'safe arrival' (in the case of goods, 'safe delivery'— the contract of carriage is not discharged until the carrier delivers the goods to the consignee undamaged). Price and quality of service, and the possibility of a pleasant view of the countryside, are incidental to this ulterior satisfaction.

Any policy concerned solely with one mode is therefore imperfect. The present dispensation still places the car, the minicab, the taxi, the bus, the coach and the train each in a different régime, and we are already seeing the appearance of another for the neologism 'Light Rapid Transit', which is in fact the apotheosis of the tramcar. Beyond that there lies the possible return of the trolleybus and, more hopefully for the continuance of the market process, the development of the busway. Yet in their capitalisation, regulation, taxation and safety control each of them exists in an isolated world of its own.

At the heart of the problem lies the issue of the transport industry's infrastructure—in railway parlance, 'track, terminals and signalling'. For half a century the argument has been over track costs, but now at last there is growing evidence that the real issue is track *pricing*. Pending the remarketisation of the whole infrastructure, by the privatisation of highways,[7] and the return of rail track investment to the capital market, electronic point-of-sale road-use pricing is as good a second-best solution as could be hoped for. It must form the corner-stone of a coherent policy for the 'mobility industry'. Only then can such coherence be extended to the other areas of confusion: investment, fiscal policy and regulation.

A Coherent Policy

Policies can now be identified which will bring down the barriers between the different modes of transport involved, and lead to a unified market for mobility. The first lies in the area of capitalisation and investment, where at present the consequences of state ownership still lead to distortions. The capital debt of the privatised bus companies varies widely, some having been bought cheap, while later sales commanded

---

[7] See J. Hibbs and G. Roth, *op. cit.*

higher prices. Time will eventually sort out these variations, but the forthcoming privatisation of British Rail will add to the complication, until such time as it is completed (and quite possibly beyond). What can be done now is to harmonise government policy for investment in railways and highways, where incompatible criteria are compounded by the use of social cost/benefit techniques, for highways alone. This, it is understood, the present Government intends to do.

Fiscal policy is the second area where radical thought is urgently required. There is general agreement that the issue of 'company cars' and their treatment as a fringe benefit requires further attention. Successive Chancellors have indeed moved (if slowly) to tackle the inequities of the tax régime, but despite the more radical changes proposed in the most recent Budget (March 1993), it remains unbalanced, and weighted against the use of public transport. It is little noted that railway staff, for example, pay tax on the imputed value of their 'travel privileges', whether or not they make use of them. Demands for tax relief for commuters' season tickets sit ill with benefits for company cars, and, as we have seen,[8] would be largely regressive. Public policy requires an integrated fiscal régime for all forms of passenger transport, including the private car.

Such a régime of course implies grasping the nettle of fuel and energy taxation, where policies for the car and for public transport so widely diverge. If the case for an element of sumptuary taxation is accepted, and that demand for car use would not respond significantly to anything less than a truly massive increase of duty, the present hydrocarbon tax is hard to criticise. It is the discrimination between the various modes of transport that raises problems for a market solution to the present imbalance of demand.

Railway transport is not currently taxed on its diesel fuel, and there is as yet no energy tax on the current used by electric trains or trams. The bus industry is allowed a rebate on tax paid for its diesel fuel, but only for registered local bus mileage.[9] There is no apparent reason why express coaches

8   See R.W.S. Pryke and J.S. Dodgson, *The Rail Problem*, London: Martin Robertson, 1975, discussed at p.31 above.

9   The obvious inefficiency of making bus companies pay tax and then claim it back is explained by the difficulties entailed in making sure a tax-free fuel does not reach unauthorised users.

should be subject to tax when the competing express trains are not, and there is a peculiar value-judgement in the implied assumption that a coach trip to the seaside or the bingo hall is less valuable to society than the local bus. The argument that Value Added Tax should be extended to fares (at present zero-rated) is likely to be settled in due course by the EC Commission; it is clearly necessary that VAT should apply to all passenger fares, including taxis and hire cars, railway and airline tickets, but if in the meantime the competitive position of public transport is improved by road pricing, the consequences should be less serious than they are currently expected to be.

Fiscal Policy—a 'Minefield of Controversy'

At the heart of the fiscal problem lies the question of how far taxes or prices can be used to internalise the externalities associated with all forms of transport. This is a minefield of controversy, involving among other things the extent to which lead-free petrol and catalytic converters increase the emission of damaging CO_2 into the atmosphere, and the increased pollution that follows from electric transport using energy obtained by raising steam, whether from nuclear or fossil fuels. The diesel engine, when properly maintained, is the most environmentally friendly means of mechanical propulsion, and fiscal policy should recognise that fact.

What is certain is that there should be a harmonised fiscal régime for all modes of transport, freight as well as passenger, so the market can encourage efficiency and, by optimising the supply of the means to mobility, enable people to maximise their marginal utility through access to the satisfactions they desire.

Competition Policy: Consolidation and Parity of Treatment

Then there is *competition policy*, in which there is still much to be done. Consolidating the regulatory régime for taxis, hire cars and buses[10] is an obvious first step, which would open the door to innovation. The taxi and hire car trade is already familiar with the franchising of drivers, and under the 1985 Transport Act, this method could be extended to the provision of minibus services; one major bus company has already diversified into taxi operation.

[10] See recommendations above, pp. 28-29.

But the necessary residual function of regulation is the maintenance of safety ('quality control') in an inherently fail-dangerous industry.[11] It is here that parity of treatment fails, when public transport is compared with the private car. Drivers of commercial vehicles are subject to a far stricter test of competence than that faced by private motorists, even though their vehicles are also subject to more exhaustive mechanical examinations than those required by the 'MOT test' for cars. Furthermore, the loss of a commercial driver's licence directly affects his employment, whereas for most car drivers it is little more than an inconvenience.

Every attempt to raise the standards of car driving has been met by highly emotional resistance, from the requirement to fit reversing mirrors through the introduction of driving tests to the imposition of the MOT test itself. But while most politicians doubtless fear that further measures would be suicidal, interfering as they must with the liberty of the subject to use a motor car, if the car is to become 'just another means of transport' it must be subject to quality controls no less stringent than those required for the rest. Speed limiters may or may not be justified for commercial vehicles (their requirement being an overtly political measure), but if a case can be made out, then it ought to apply equally to the private car.

Competition policy, in short, must not be limited to the bus industry. So far as quality control is concerned, the balance is tilted too far in favour of the private car. The statistics in Table 8 show how much safer it is to travel by public transport, and if a quality threshold is justified at all, it should surely apply to all modes.

Finally, there is unfinished business left over from the Ridley reforms, including some questions as to how they have worked in practice. The first concerns the politically contentious issue of the impact of subsidy policy on the market for bus transport. This takes two forms: the provision of so-called 'socially necessary' services by tender[12] and the availability of reduced fares for 'senior citizens' and the disabled, both provided for in the 1985 Act.

Though there is very little data, references in the trade press make clear that policies vary considerably between

[11] See above, page 53.
[12] See above, page 54-55.

TABLE 8

PASSENGER CASUALTY RATES: BY MODE OF TRANSPORT, GREAT BRITAIN, Average, 1981-1990

(Per billion passenger-kms.)

Mode	Killed	KSI*	All severities
Air[1]	0·2	0·3	0·4
Rail	1·0	3·6	74·0
Water[2]	10·0	46·0	••
Bus or coach	0·5	18·0	198·0
Car or van[3]	4·8	64·0	339·0
Two-wheeled motor vehicle[4]	106·0	2,138·0	6,892·0
Pedal cycle	50·0	958·0	4,780·0
Pedestrian	72·0	738·0	2,425·0

*KSI: Killed or severely injured.   •• = Not available

Notes:
[1] World passenger-carrying services of UK airlines for fixed and rotary wing aircraft over 2,300 kilograms.
[2] Domestic and international passenger services of UK-registered vessels.
[3] Car drivers, car and van passengers in Great Britain.
[4] Drivers and passengers in Great Britain.

Source: Transport Statistics Great Britain 1992, London: HMSO, 1992, Table 1.8.

different authorities, and that the load factor on tendered services may be exceptionally low. The real problem, however, is the combination of vote-seeking and rent-seeking[13] behaviour that is inescapably opposed to regulatory reform.

[13] 'Rent-seeking', which is characteristic of the market for regulation, is the extraction from public organisations of 'rent', defined as reward over and above that which would be provided by discriminating consumers in a competitive market: see J.M. Buchanan, R.D. Tollison and G. Tullock, *Towards a Theory of the Rent-Seeking Society*, Texas A&M University Press, 1980 (quoted in A. Seldon, *Capitalism*, Oxford: Blackwell, 1990, p.162). Its extent was shown by the shake-out in staff (mainly managers at all levels) that followed privatisation.

In the provision of services that are assumed to be socially necessary one encounters the concept of 'social justice', which is a political rather than an ethical or economic concept.[14] Yet the argument cuts across party boundaries, and the real issue must be the extent to which subsidies are justified by or arise out of market failure. In the absence of rigorous investigation, the jury is still out but, in general, subsidy policy inhibits the ability of the market to supply all forms of mobility.

The present system of providing 'socially necessary' bus services is inherently anti-competitive, and obstructs the working of the market. It is justified by the appeal to 'social justice' that Hayek has criticised so trenchantly,[15] and it is in all probability regressive in its impact.[16] There is every reason to suppose it to be unnecessary, except perhaps in rural areas as a last resort. In such cases it would be best to place subsidy powers and finances in the hands of Parish Councils, whose members could enter into a contract with a local bus firm for the supply of their felt need. What is most urgent is a study of existing practices, to identify the amount of 'fresh air' that is being carried about at the taxpayers' expense.

User-subsidy for senior citizens raises wider issues, affecting urban mobility and the urban transport market. It is discriminatory in so far as it does not extend to the taxi and private car hire trade, which is in many ways better suited to the carriage of many older people.[17] To satisfy the appropriate lobby, the 1985 Act gave powers to local authorities to provide concessionary fare schemes for senior citizens, subject to their being open to any operator in the district to take part. One criticism is that such schemes make subsidy available to people whose financial situation makes subsidy unjustified. In practice, because of the low social status of the bus, many people would not wish to be identified by holding a 'pensioner's pass', but with

[14] See above, page 63.

[15] *Ibid.*

[16] See above, page 55.

[17] Bus conductors are remembered for greater 'customer care' than the *macho* bus driver, who moves away from the stop before his (the gender is deliberate) passengers have been able to find a seat.

the move up the market that must follow from road pricing, this proposition might well be undermined.

How far can the market itself provide for the needs of the less well-off citizen, without the administrative costs to the public purse? There must presumably be competitive advantages in price discrimination of this kind.[18] One needs only to look at the pensioners' reduced fares on offer by British Rail, with no compensating subsidy, to see what the market can provide, and everywhere there are hairdressers and television rental firms, for instance, offering special rates to pensioners, too. In the food trade, cut-price chains such as Aldi play an important part in maintaining the standard of living of people (of all ages) on low incomes, without asking for any support from public funds. (Indeed, councils are sometimes besought to refuse such firms planning permission, on the ground that they are a threat to established chains or to branded manufacturers.) In the absence of public subsidy any bus company that took the sensible commercial decision to offer reduced fares off-peak to pensioners and other 'disadvantaged' citizens would start a chain reaction, as other firms found it desirable to do the same.

Price Wars and the OFT's Policies

Much here depends upon the realisation among bus company managers that price and quality form an area for marketing initiatives, and that they need not be the cause of debilitating price wars. There is a need for the Office of Fair Trading to review its policies towards the bus industry[19] (not least the way it views travelcards). The OFT has also inhibited the provision of co-ordinated publicity by different firms, though it has to be said that the record of the industry as a whole leaves much to be desired in the area of marketing management. The OFT may yet require powers for dealing firmly with predatory behaviour which inhibits the entrepreneurial challenge of new and smaller firms.[20]

[18] The advent of the 'decremental chip card' (see above, page 62) will make such discrimination both easier and more tactful.

[19] See above, pp. 65-67.

[20] See above, pp. 67-68. Perhaps in time bus company managers will cease to regard new competitors as a threat to 'their' passengers—as if any firm could be said to 'own' its customers.

One or two adjustments then remain to be made, if the market is to be as free as possible to satisfy demand. The need to register local bus services, which was no doubt justified when the consequences of regulatory reform were seen to be problematic, has now gone, and the '42-day rule' should be rescinded. The system does little more than to consume paper wastefully and to take up executives' time that could be better spent in other ways. If there is to be provision of replacements at public expense where commercial services are withdrawn, then a requirement that such an intention be advertised in a local newspaper of record should suffice (and would in any case be good public relations). And steps should be immediately taken to prevent the absurd claim that property rights inhere in route numbers[21] from inhibiting competition.

Finally, there is the impact of highway planning, where conventional wisdom may still run contrary to the necessity to provide a freely working market for mobility. On the one hand, there is the case for bus priority schemes, which the Department of Transport and the Bus & Coach Council are currently publicising. They should be extended to allow for busways and other specialised provision,[22] which must be provided in such a way as to be open to all to use them (after investing in the necessary equipment). But on the other hand there is the danger that 'traffic calming'[23] policies may be used to discourage innovation, and lead to the unilateral development of pedestrianised areas, to the disadvantage of the bus. This is an area in which local planners may be criticised for failing to recognise the importance of mobility, while the industry, through privatisation, has lost what limited status it had in the local planning process. Steps ought to be taken to restore the balance.

Above all, the bus industry does not need a return to the paternalism of local government, and neither does it need artificially engineered competition, using public funds, from schemes for Light Rapid Transit, devised to give more power

---

[21] See above, pp. 66-67.

[22] See above, Box 1, pp. 36-37.

[23] The provision of 'humps' (so-called 'sleeping policemen') and 'chicanes' that make it difficult to operate buses (and emergency vehicles) in residential streets.

to administrators and politicians. There is no halfway house here; no 'social market'. Its greatest need is to become more entrepreneurial, and markedly to improve its marketing management. That is its own affair, and the Bus and Coach Council is well aware of the problem. While local authority planners will have to learn to respect the bus as the mode of transport that uses scarce road space economically, it would be disastrous if they were to regain control of operations, and use the bus (as some no doubt would like) to clobber the motorist.

An Integrated Market for Mobility

It is more than 20 years since the significance of road pricing for the market was identified, when *The Economist* wrote:

> '[I]f road-pricing was introduced, the price it would exact from private motorists would revolutionise the competitiveness of buses, which would then be able to invest in improved services. . . . Then, it might even be possible to abolish bus monopolies.'[24]

That percipient observation, so many years ahead of its time, expresses the central argument of this *Hobart Paper*. If there is to be a unified market for mobility, comprising every mode of public transport and the private car,[25] then allowing the bus a fair run must be the primary measure of reform. The opportunity to do this was missed in the Transport Act 1985, though the present author had argued that road pricing was a *sine qua non* for a functioning market for bus services themselves.[26] Inter-modal competition between the bus and the car is central to the issue, and such reform should be the starting point for harmonising the regulatory, investment and fiscal régimes for the various players in the market. Only in this way can there be formulated the 'national transport policy' so often called for.[27]

[24] 'What was that about bus services?', *The Economist*, 27 March 1971.

[25] This admittedly neglects walking and cycling which are substitutes for other forms of transport, each of which requires highway engineering and consequent investment. Their importance should not be ignored.

[26] See Hibbs, *Transport Without Politics. . .?*, *op. cit.*, p.62.

[27] Judith Hanna and Martin Mogridge, in *Travel Sickness* (London: Lawrence & Wishart, 1992) argue cogently for an integrated market (Chapter 9, 'Market Forces and Transport Choices'), but envisage a degree of intervention which would require information it seems we would be unable to obtain—quite apart from our lack of data as to the initial situation (see above, page 79).

VI. CONCLUSION—IMPROVING THE MARKET

Many people who observe the results of spontaneous order, cannot conceive that it was not planned. Undeterred by the experience of planned transport, at home and abroad, they still seek a 'national transport policy' that entails a central bureaucracy charged with the impossible duty of deciding what is best. Those who point to the element of waste to be found in any market—an inevitable consequence of inability to forecast the future accurately—should look to the misallocation of public funds that required the Beeching reforms for the railways, and the Ridley reforms for the buses. And they should contemplate the waste involved in the ways cars are used, which is a consequence of insulating roads from the allocatory functions of the market.

If there is to be a national transport policy, its application to people movement should be to ensure that consumers' decisions are made within a market which extends to all forms of physical mobility.[1] Anything else will favour one or another mode, or some particular group of people, at the expense of others, and it will usually be the poor who suffer. A necessary condition for such a market is that suppliers' decisions are taken on what has come to be called 'a level playing field'.

It has been argued in this *Hobart Paper* that the harmonisation of fiscal and investment régimes across the spectrum of transport modes is an urgent priority, centering on the introduction of a pricing system for the use of congested road space, and the return of road and rail infrastructure investments to the discipline of the capital market. One aspect of this is the need for a critical examination of all proposals for Light Rapid Transit, which are liable to be tainted by political priorities and vote-seeking behaviour. The 'low-tech' alternative of KGB (kerb-guided buses) has two important advantages: it is far cheaper (and requires less land), and it need not interfere with the market process.

---

[1] It is likely that the market will be extended quite soon by developments in information technology.

Regulatory reform and privatisation in the bus industry has been proceeding for 12 years now. A few loose ends require to be tidied up—not the least being the competition policy of the Office of Fair Trading. But, contrary to much conventional wisdom, the Ridley reforms have not proved a disaster. Criticisms made by the Association of Metropolitan Authorities need to be set against the experience of towns and cities previously served by subsidiaries of the National Bus Company. Bus companies have a long way to go in developing marketing management. Nevertheless, their future is not unduly bleak, and it would be transformed by the introduction of road-use pricing.

On regulation, much could be done to unify the market for mobility. Because transport is 'fail-dangerous' it must be subject to quality control, but whereas the safety regulations for buses are sometimes obscurantist, the standards required for driving and maintaining private cars are absurdly lax. The regulation of the taxi trade, including hire cars (sometimes called minicabs), is out of date, and radical reform is required. There is always a need to oversee safety regulations so as to avoid unnecessary restrictions on innovation and freedom to compete, and in this area a critical eye should be kept on the current fashions for pedestrianisation and traffic calming.

The paper started with a reference to Kipling's remark that 'transport is civilisation'. Freedom of movement—or 'mobility'—is a basic requirement for civil society. It is no business of planners or managers to question the reason why people want to travel (apart from genuine market research). It is enough that mobility is desired as a means of access to other satisfactions. So when it comes to people's choice of mode, they will derive most satisfaction if they can choose what serves them best within the overall optimising function of an unencumbered market process.

Consequently, no one mode of transport must be given an advantage over the rest by the way fiscal, investment and regulatory policies work. Even though each has its own culture, managers as well as customers must come to see each mode as 'just another form of transport'. If that is hard for committed railway, bus or taxi people to accept, how much harder is it for those committed to the use of the private car!

It is 'politically correct' in some circles to stigmatise the private car. There is an element of hypocrisy in this, for the car is increasingly to be found in the ownership of lower income groups because of the way it extends opportunities for employment. There is, too, an element of nostalgia that runs through much public debate about the railways. It lies behind the attraction of Light Rapid Transit. If, on balance, this paper calls for a pro-public transport policy, that must be seen as part of an overall commitment to extending the market for personal mobility. The alternative is the not unfashionable prescription that would constrain the use of cars by direct intervention, while returning public transport to centralised, bureaucratic control.

QUESTIONS FOR DISCUSSION

1. Account for the neglect of the private car, seen simply as a means of transport, in the broad sphere of Transport Studies.

2. What would be the disadvantages of using fuel tax as a means of bringing home to motorists the external costs associated with running a car?

3. Is there any over-riding objection to bringing taxis and hire cars into the same regulatory framework?

4. Account for the disparity between the small proportion of total traffic that is carried by rail in the UK and the high profile of railways in public debate.

5. What may be the reasons why Light Rapid Transit has been described as 'a solution looking for a problem'?

6. To what extent have the Transport Acts of 1980 and 1985 succeeded in returning the bus industry to the market?

7. Was Mr Prescott right when he said of deregulation that 'All in all it's been pretty bloody disastrous'?

8. Why should road-use pricing be seen as a great marketing opportunity for the bus industry?

9. Account for the generally uncritical assumption that there are 'socially necessary' bus and train services in the UK, which the market will not of itself provide.

10. 'Harmonised regulatory, investment and fiscal régimes for all modes form the only meaningful basis for a "national transport policy".' Do you agree, or disagree, and why?

FURTHER READING

Banister, D. and K. Button (eds.), *Transport in a Free Market Economy*, London: Macmillan, 1991.

Bayliss, D. *et al.*, *Paying for Progress, A Report on Congestion and Road Use Charges*, London: Chartered Institute of Transport, 1990. Also supplementary report, 1992.

Bayliss, D. *et al.*, *Transport Options for London*, Greater London Group, London School of Economics, 1992.

Beesley, M.E., *Privatisation, Regulation and Deregulation*, London: Routledge, in association with the Institute of Economic Affairs, 1992.

Bell, P. and P. Cloke (eds.), *Deregulation and Transport—Market Forces in the Modern World*, London: David Fulton Publishers, 1990.

Button, K. and D. Pitfield (eds.), *Transport Deregulation—An International Movement*, London: Macmillan, 1991.

Goodwin, P. *et al.*, *Bus Deregulation in the Metropolitan Areas*, Aldershot: Avebury, 1991.

Foster, C.D., *Privatisation, Public Ownership and the Regulation of Natural Monopoly*, Oxford: Blackwell, 1992.

Hibbs, J. and G. Roth, *Tomorrow's Way—Managing Roads in a Free Society*, London: Adam Smith Institute, 1992.

Kay, J. *et al.* (eds.), *Privatisation and Regulation—the UK Experience*, Oxford: Clarendon Press, 1986.

Kilvington, R.P., and A.K. Cross, *Deregulation of Express Coach Services in Britain*, Aldershot: Gower, 1986.

Savage, I., *The Deregulation of Bus Services*, Aldershot: Gower, 1985.

Truelove, P., *Decision Making in Transport Planning*, London: Longman, 1992.

Veljanovski, C. (ed.), *Privatisation and Competition—A Market Prospectus*, Hobart Paperback No.28, London: Institute of Economic Affairs, 1989.

Can De-Industrialisation
Seriously Damage Your Wealth?
N.F.R. CRAFTS

In Hobart Paper No. 120, Professor Nick Crafts, a distinguished economic historian from the University of Warwick, examines the evidence about growth rates in Britain as compared with other countries and also considers the case for an 'industrial policy' which promotes British manufacturing industry.

He demonstrates the long-term nature of relative economic decline in Britain, but he shows also that there was some revival in the 1980s (especially of manufacturing output). The main 'industrial' problem which emerged in the 1980s was a significant deterioration in the manufacturing trade balance. Some economists have claimed that government should help manufacturers by subsidies for investment, protection for 'infant industries' and intervention to correct 'market failures'—in other words, a return to the policy of 'picking winners' which operated in the 1960s and 1970s when relative economic decline was at its worst.

Professor Crafts shows that the relatively slow growth of the British economy up to 1979 was a consequence of an environment which encouraged the survival of the inefficient. Under the Thatcher administrations of the 1980s, however, some of the obstacles to growth were diminished and the '. . . UK performed a somewhat belated catching-up exercise associated with the switch in policy régime'. Although there is scope for eliminating policy errors by government, Professor Crafts argues that interventionist industrial policies may well impose costs which exceed any benefits they bring.

Productivity growth was significantly increased in the Thatcher years and it is therefore 'important not to return to the *status quo ante* 1979'. Intervention is only too likely to reduce the pressure on firms to reduce costs. Professor Crafts sees scope for government action to 'reduce short-termism and to strengthen human capital formation' but he warns that such action should ensure that the 'disciplines of competition' are retained.

ISBN 0-255 36316-8

Hobart Paper 120

The Institute of Economic Affairs
2 Lord North Street, Westminster
London SW1P 3LB
Telephone: 071-799 3745

£8.95